CultureShock!
A Survival Guide to Customs and Etiquette

Netherlands

Hunt Janin
Ria van Eil

Marshall Cavendish
Editions

This edition published in 2008 by:
Marshall Cavendish Corporation
99 White Plains Road
Tarrytown, NY 10591-9001
www.marshallcavendish.us

Other Marshall Cavendish Offices:
Marshall Cavendish International (Asia) Private Limited. 1 New Industrial Road, Singapore 536196 ■ Marshall Cavendish Ltd. 5th Floor, 32–38 Saffron Hill, London EC1N 8FH, UK ■ Marshall Cavendish International (Thailand) Co Ltd. 253 Asoke, 12th Flr, Sukhumvit 21 Road, Klongtoey Nua, Wattana, Bangkok 10110, Thailand ■ Marshall Cavendish (Malaysia) Sdn Bhd, Times Subang, Lot 46, Subang Hi-Tech Industrial Park, Batu Tiga, 40000 Shah Alam, Selangor Darul Ehsan, Malaysia

Marshall Cavendish is a trademark of Times Publishing Limited

ISBN 10: 0-7614-5492-6
ISBN 13: 978-0-7614-5492-2

Please contact the publisher for the Library of Congress catalog number

Printed in China by Everbest Printing Co Ltd

Photo Credits:
All black and white photos by Hunt Janin except page 12 (Ria van eil); pages viii, 5, 6, 42, 67, 98, 117, 130, 135, 137, 141 (Corel Stock Photo Library); page 65 (Getty Images); page 89 (Schiphol Airport); page 145 (the M.C. Esther Company); and pages 47, 71, 110, 118, 120, 132, 154, 155, 189, 216 (Pietro Scòzzari). Colour photos from Photolibrary pages d–e, l–m; Getty Images pages a, b, c, f–g, h, j–k, n–o, p. ■ Cover photo: Photolibrary.

All illustrations by TRIGG

ABOUT THE SERIES

Culture shock is a state of disorientation that can come over anyone who has been thrust into unknown surroundings, away from one's comfort zone. *CultureShock!* is a series of trusted and reputed guides which has, for decades, been helping expatriates and long-term visitors to cushion the impact of culture shock whenever they move to a new country.

Written by people who have lived in the country and experienced culture shock themselves, the authors share all the information necessary for anyone to cope with these feelings of disorientation more effectively. The guides are written in a style that is easy to read and covers a range of topics that will arm readers with enough advice, hints and tips to make their lives as normal as possible again.

Each book is structured in the same manner. It begins with the first impressions that visitors will have of that city or country. To understand a culture, one must first understand the people—where they came from, who they are, the values and traditions they live by, as well as their customs and etiquette. This is covered in the first half of the book.

Then on with the practical aspects—how to settle in with the greatest of ease. Authors walk readers through how to find accommodation, get the utilities and telecommunications up and running, enrol the children in school and keep in the pink of health. But that's not all. Once the essentials are out of the way, venture out and try the food, enjoy more of the culture and travel to other areas. Then be immersed in the language of the country before discovering more about the business side of things.

To round off, snippets of basic information are offered before readers are 'tested' on customs and etiquette of the country. Useful words and phrases, a comprehensive resource guide and list of books for further research are also included for easy reference.

CONTENTS

FOREWORD

In 1780, John Adams, who was then the American envoy to the *Staten-Generaal* (the 'States General', i.e. the Dutch parliament) and who later became the second President of the United States, wrote home to his wife:

> 'I am very much pleased with Holland. It is a singular country. It is like no other... The frugality, industry, cleanliness, etc. here deserve the imitation of my countrymen.'

Today, more than two centuries later, the Netherlands is still a singular country like no other. We hope that *CultureShock! Netherlands* will give you a useful introduction to what has aptly been called the 'country of mild happiness'.

This book would not have been possible without the help of many Dutch men, women and even children.

We cannot thank all of them but do want to acknowledge the excellent comments and suggestions from Petronella van Gorkom, Dr Marie-Charlotte LeBailly, Dr Hans Cools and Johanna van Fessem. Every effort has been made to ensure that the information presented here is accurate. But conditions do change and we strongly urge anyone who is planning to visit, live or work in the Netherlands to check first with the nearest Netherlands embassy or consulate or with other competent Dutch authorities to get the latest word on rules and regulations.

MAP OF THE NETHERLANDS

NORTH SEA

AMSTERDAM

NETHERLANDS

GERMANY

BELGIUM

Tulips—the pride of the Netherlands.

A LAND OF SKY AND WATER

Denkend aan Holland	Thinking of Holland
zie ik brede rivieren	I see wide rivers
traag door oneindig	Winding lazily through
laagland gaan...	endless low countryside...
en in de geweldige	And farmhouses, low and lost
ruimte verzonken de	In the immense open space...
boerderijen...	

—Poem by Hendrik Marsman (1899–1945)

VAST UNINTERRUPTED SKIES, ENORMOUS CLOUDSCAPES, a soft ever-changing light, and everywhere you look, **water**—rivers, lakes, canals, locks, ponds, *slootjes* (narrow drainage ditches) and the North Sea; these will be some of your first impressions. Almost 20 per cent of the Netherlands consists of water.

Even if you are not a landscape artist, you will still appreciate the quiet beauty of this well-ordered country. And when you spend some time here, you will also be favourably impressed by the tall, prosperous and above all, highly competent people who inhabit it. This competence is reflected in the fact that the Dutch have won 15 Nobel prizes in such diverse fields as chemistry, physics, medicine, economics and peace-making.

The small scale of things, the flatness of the land, the large number of bicycles, the relative absence of poverty, the rush-hour traffic gridlock, and the density of the population will strike you too. The Dutch will not be slow to complain to you about their labyrinthine maze of rules and regulations. You will gradually find, however, that these bureaucratic constraints are, in fact, one of the things that makes the Netherlands such an equitable society and such a good place to live and work today.

You will notice that the Netherlands is a small, very densely populated country of about 17 million people, located on the North Sea on the delta of three major rivers: the Rhine, Maas, and Scheldt. It is often called 'Holland' because in the 17th

In the Netherlands, you are never very far from water.

century, the former province of Holland was economically and politically dominant. Officially, however, the country today is referred to as the Netherlands rather than Holland.

The term Netherlands is not only more accurate but also conveys an essential fact about the country. As the Dutch words *neder* (low) and *landen* (lands) suggest, it is indeed low-lying. Today, about 27 per cent of the country is below sea level and if all the dykes and dunes were breached, much of the most densely populated part of the country would quickly be flooded by the rivers and the sea.

It's Just Not Possible!

The famous children's story about Hans Brinker, who used his finger to plug a leak in a dyke until help could come, is less known in the Netherlands than in Britain or the US, probably because it is too far-fetched. As Han van der Horst explains in *The Low Sky*, when a dyke gives way, it takes much more than a boy's finger to stop it. The reason: "The water comes like a wall… boring a deep hole in the ground immediately behind the dyke. It then spreads out, thundering and boiling, sweeping away everything in its path— trees, cattle, people…" The Netherlands owes its very existence to continuous heavy-duty feats of hydraulic engineering. Nevertheless, there is a statue of Hans in the small village of Spaarndam (not far from Haarlem), where his dyke-plugging feat is supposed to have occurred.

The Dutch are world travellers and world traders. You will quickly discover that most of them are tolerant. They usually like foreign visitors, foreign languages, foreign food and foreign things. Linguistically, you may be in for a very pleasant surprise. If you ask a Dutch man or woman on the street a question in a language other than Dutch, he or she may well reply in English, or even in your own language!

Each of the Netherlands' major cities has its distinctive character, even though they are not very far apart. The 'big four'—Amsterdam, The Hague, Rotterdam and Utrecht—are all part of an urban conurbation known as the Randstad, which has a population of ten million. Our own favourite city is Amsterdam. This is the most popular destination for foreign visitors because of its famous museums (notably the Rijksmuseum and the Van Gogh Museum), its ring of canals

This zebra clock is located in the Hague.

As Princess Maxima once exclaimed,
the Netherlands is "...full of flowers".

with stately mansions (best seen from the water by canal boat), and its multicultural atmosphere of endless freedom and ceaseless creativity. Cities such as The Hague, Delft, Haarlem, Utrecht, Groningen and Maastricht have their own share of historic buildings, museums, traditions and attractions too. You will also discover many picture-postcard-perfect villages in the countryside.

Princess Maxima, now the wife of Crown Prince Willem-Alexander, had one of the most pleasant initial impressions ever recorded when she first arrived in the Netherlands in 1999 from her native Argentina. During a 2005 interview on Dutch television, she remembered that: "Everything was so clean, full of flowers." She saw a woman on a bicycle who, in keeping with a good Dutch tradition, had one child on a seat at the front of the bike, another child on a seat at the back, and was carrying some shopping bags as well. Princess Maxima was so astounded by what is a familiar sight in the Netherlands that she said to Crown Prince Willem-Alexander, "I could never do that!"

'I saw the danger to the land... the gaps in the dyke
were jagged and dangerous because much of it had
fallen into a deep breach. In the early morning I sent
the drummer around to summon every person to work.
Those women who had no barrows carried clay in their
aprons; others carried it in sacks on their shoulders;
still others made bundles of sticks... I managed to
collect a large number of people and in the end
we succeeded fully in repairing the breach.'
—Andries Vierlingh, dyke-master for the princes of Orange,
on how he dealt with a breach in the dyke.

THE NETHERLANDS IS CONVENIENTLY LOCATED on the western edge of the Eurasian land mass—on the North Sea and at the estuaries of the Rhine, the Maas and the Scheldt rivers. It is flanked by Belgium on the south and south-west and by Germany on the east. The United Kingdom is roughly 160 km (100 miles) to the west, on the other side of the shallow, choppy North Sea. Much appreciated by many Dutch travellers, *la douce France* ('sweet France') is about the same distance to the south-west, on the other side of Belgium.

A LANDSCAPE SHAPED BY HUMAN HANDS

Nearly everything under the luminous Dutch sky is man-made and tailored to human measure. There are no Alps, Grand Canyons, Sahara Deserts or vast forests here. What you will find instead is a small-scaled but very charming tapestry, geometrically woven of carefully maintained cities, villages, canals, polders, lakes, roads, bridges, farmhouses and meticulously cultivated fields.

Foreign visitors have always been favourably impressed by the Netherlands. An 18th century Italian historian commented on the cleanliness of the villages and the neatness of the countryside. In the same era, Sachaverall Stevens, an English gentleman, was enthusiastic about his own travels from Utrecht to Amsterdam 'along one of the most agreeable roads in all Europe', which he said was like 'an avenue in the best laid out garden'. With the exception of some inner city districts, most of the Netherlands is still impeccably clean and neat today.

The population density of about 465 inhabitants per sq km (or 1,202 per sq mile) is one of the highest in the world —about 20 times that of the US and twice that of the UK. This is due not so much to excessive numbers of people as to the small size of the country itself. The Netherlands is only 310 km (193 miles) from north to south. Including such major bodies of water as the Waddenzee (*zee* means sea) off the province of Friesland and the freshwater IJsselmeer (*meer* means lake) between Friesland, Flevoland and North Holland, it has a total area of about 42,696 sq km (16,485 sq miles) and is just a little bigger than nearby Belgium.

HIGHS AND LOWS

The Dutch are the first to admit that most of the Netherlands is *zo plat als een pannenkoek* ('as flat as a pancake'). Compared with neighbouring countries, there is not much geographical diversity here. The highest point is Drielandenpunt on the southern tip of the country, where the German and Belgian frontiers meet. It boasts an elevation of 322 m (1,056 ft). There are also a few low hills, initially composed of debris left by glaciers which retreated a million years ago, in the

Its flat countryside makes the Netherlands perfect for bicycle trips.

Utrechtse Heuvelrug south-east of Utrecht and in the Veluwe west of Apeldoorn.

At the opposite end of the spectrum, the lowest point in the Netherlands is near Rotterdam—at Nieuwerkerk aan de IJssel, more than -6.74 m (22 ft) below sea level.

REGIONS OF THE NETHERLANDS
The West
A broad featureless plain in the western part of the country, originally composed of marine and river-borne clays, is now the most densely populated region. Known as the Randstad, it contains the four major cities of the Netherlands—Amsterdam, Rotterdam, The Hague and Utrecht—and is home to more than ten million people. The Randstad is at best only a few feet above sea level, so if all the dykes and dams broke, most of it would soon be under water—as would Schiphol, the Netherlands' splendid international airport, which is more than 4.3 m (14 ft) below sea level and was formerly part of the bed of Haarlem Lake.

The South-west
In the south-west, four big rivers (the Rhine, Maas, Waal and Scheldt) in the provinces of South Holland and Zeeland flow into the North Sea and have formed estuaries, islands and a wide, flat delta there. This area was especially vulnerable to flooding and is now the site of the huge Delta Works. In southern Limburg, the flat Dutch plains—now pleasant fertile landscapes highlighted by manor houses and old farms—give rise to the Ardennes hills of Belgium.

The North and the East
The northern and eastern parts of the Netherlands border on Germany and are much more rural than the Randstad, although population and industrialisation are increasing in this predominantly agricultural area as well. But the pace of life here is still slower than in Amsterdam or Rotterdam and the inhabitants are not given to as many words.

The cultural attractions of these regions include some of the medieval commercial ports (such as Staveren and

Kampen), south of Groningen, the *hunebeds*—prehistoric burial chambers which date from 2000 BC.

The northern province of Friesland offers truly excellent outdoor recreation. The best activity in summer is boating—sailing, cruising under power or simply rowing on the many lakes and rivers. Many Dutch people simply love the water and are excellent with all vessels, large and small.

The best outdoor activity in the winter is skating. On the rare occasions when a really cold winter freezes the canals hard enough, the famous *Elfstedentocht* (Eleven Towns Tour) is held. This begins in icy darkness at 5:30 am and goes through 11 Frisian towns along a 199-km-long (123-mile-long) course. Extra trains have to be laid on in the Netherlands to bring tens of thousands of spectators to watch the 300 or so competitive skaters and the roughly 14,000 touring skaters who tackle this demanding course. The winner always becomes a national hero.

DUNES, DYKES, POLDERS AND CANALS

Hydraulic engineering (i.e. water management) is the single most important factor in shaping the Dutch landscape. Natural sand dunes along the coast have been planted with tough grasses to stabilise them. These play an essential role

Beach grasses help to stabilise the sand dunes along the coast.

Muskrats can seriously weaken dykes by burrowing into them. This muskrat trapper is employed by the Dutch government.

in protecting inland areas from high tides and are off-limits to hikers.

Where necessary, the dunes are backed up by dykes, which the Dutch have been making since 500 BC, when the Frisians first piled up rudimentary mounds of dirt known as *terpen* and lived on them like castaway sailors. These early peoples must have had a very hard life (in AD 50, the Roman naturalist Pliny described them as a 'wretched race') but by the year 1200, the Frisians were building the first true dykes and creating the first polders (land reclaimed from the sea).

The Dutch came close to losing their war against the water in the 13th century when 35 big floods swept over low-lying areas, creating the Zuiderzee in 1287. But their brilliant response to this threat was the windmill, which could slowly but surely lift huge amounts of water and thus transform submerged or soggy areas into dry, productive

The windmill has helped transform the Dutch countryside and remains an internationally recognised symbol of the country.

polders—always good sites for farms, houses, cities and (much later) factories and airports.

The first drainage windmill was built in the Netherlands in 1414. After the devastating St Elizabeth's Day Flood of 1421—which is said to have killed 10,000 people and submerged 20 villages—many more windmills were put into operation. In the 17th century, helped by 43 windmills, the great hydraulic engineer Jan Adriaenszoon Leeghwater (appropriately enough, his surname means 'empty water') created polders to the north of Amsterdam. A network of drainage canals, their water levels carefully regulated by windmills, crisscrossed the polders and kept the water at bay.

The climate is changing. The temperature is rising and there is more precipitation, especially in the winter, so water levels are higher than before. In the summer, droughts are expected to lower the level of inland waters. Due to global warming and increasing urbanisation, flood control in the Netherlands will become more and more important in the years ahead. The Dutch have already adopted a very clear policy to guide their work: "Water must be allowed space —before it takes it for itself!"

CREATING LAND FROM WATER

The process of land reclamation picked up speed in the 19th and 20th centuries. Haarlem Lake was drained in four years, beginning in 1848, and after the floods of 1916, the Zuiderzee was transformed into the IJssel Lake by a barrier dam completed in 1932. To prevent a recurrence of the disastrous 1953 flood, the Delta Plan was drawn up. This ambitious project reached a dramatic point in 1986, when Queen Beatrix inaugurated a storm-surge barrier in the Eastern Scheldt. At extremely high tides, this huge dam, which is about 3.2 km (2 miles) long and based on two artificial islands, regulates in an environmentally sensitive way the flow of the water in an estuary 8.9 km (5.5 miles) wide and 4.6 m (115 ft) deep.

Here is the Dutch success story in hydraulic engineering: since the 13th century, the Dutch have managed to wrest from the water about 9,896 sq km (3,820 sq miles) of dry land. Large-scale land reclamation, however, has now come to an end. The shallow Waddenzee in the north of the country could be easily drained but it is an important sanctuary for birds and seals. Given the very strong Dutch commitment to protecting the environment, there is very little chance that it will ever be reclaimed.

CLIMATE OF THE NETHERLANDS

Located so close to the North Sea, the Netherlands has a cool maritime climate with the four seasons common to northern European lands. Damp, mild, and sometimes foggy, it is rarely Arctic-cold—winter temperatures average only about 2.7°C (37°F)—but there is often a stiff wind and the wind chill factor can make it seem much, much colder. Snowfalls are usually light and occur only on average 28 days per year. Frozen ponds (and sometimes the canals themselves) provide truly excellent skating.

Summers are moderate and are ideal for sailing and other water sports, with temperatures averaging about 18°C (65°F). On an average day, three-fifths of the sky is clouded and there are only about 25 perfectly clear days each year; but on the remaining days, fantastic cloudscapes usually highlight the deep blue sky.

Alas, this is a damp climate and not all days are fair: the annual average rainfall of about 88 cm (35 inches) is distributed fairly evenly throughout the year, though it tends to be higher in autumn.

Be Prepared

A Dutch lady once said, "There is no such thing as bad weather. There is just bad clothing." This is a very good point. Officially, the climate of the Netherlands may be maritime and temperate but in practice, it is also quite changeable. The well-prepared visitor will therefore bring warm, layered, windproof clothing for autumn and winter and will have rain gear and a sweater close at hand for the rest of the year.

A QUICK LOOK AT DUTCH HISTORY

The Netherlands is a very small country but its history is long and complex. Any summary of it must be highly selective and will probably appal professional historians. But as a newcomer, you really cannot hope to understand the Netherlands of today unless you have at least a faint idea about the Netherlands of the past.

To make this task easier, let us see if we can find a common thread which will help make sense of a history which stretches back at least to 30,000 BC. At the risk of great oversimplification, we can say that although Dutch history prior to the reign of Philip the Good (1396–1467) may not have a single unifying theme, later on we can indeed detect one—namely, the gradual movement towards greater national and personal freedom.

The movement towards more freedom still continues today. In fact, it has always provided an inspiration to other peoples. As Benjamin Franklin, the 18th-century American statesman and inventor, put it, "In love of liberty and in the defence of it, Holland has been our example."

Prehistory

The first faint traces of human settlement in the Netherlands date from about 30,000 BC. By 9000 BC, Stone Age hunters and fishermen equipped with flint tools were eking out a precarious existence in what is now the Netherlands.

The first human settlements date from 5300 BC, when farmers and cattle herders settled in the south near Limburg. In the north of the country, men and women, known from their pottery as the Funnelneck Beaker people, buried their dead in massive rock tombs called *hunebeds*. Weapons and tools were made of bronze by 2100 BC and of iron by 700 BC. Farmers settled along the North Sea coast on artificial mounds (*terpen*) built to keep their settlements above the flood waters.

The Romans

Julius Caesar began subjugating the Celtic and Germanic tribes of the area in 57 BC. Roman roads built along raised river banks were the next dykes and Roman forts later became the towns of Maastricht and Nijmegen. But in the 3rd century AD, Roman power began to ebb. After the legions were withdrawn, Anglos and Saxons settled in the north and east of the Netherlands, mixing with the local Frisians.

Merovingians, Carolingians and Vikings

The Franks, a Germanic people, became the dominant group in the early Middle Ages. The most successful Merovingian king, Clovis (AD 466–511), conquered all of Gaul (France). In AD 695, the Pope appointed the Anglo-Saxon missionary Willibrord to be archbishop of the Frisians and bishop of Utrecht, but Christianity spread slowly in the northern Netherlands.

The Merovingians were overthrown by Pepin II, who established the Carolingian dynasty, named after his famous son, Charlemagne, who succeeded him in AD 768. Charlemagne reigned for 47 years and expanded his realm to such an extent that he was crowned in Rome as the Holy Roman Emperor. The social structure gradually changed as feudalism began to bind lords to their king, who gave them land in return for their military and financial support. These lords in turn granted land to their own vassals, who lived on the labour of the bondsmen (peasants) who were tied to the soil and who tilled the fields.

Vikings, those fierce sea-loving Norsemen, repeatedly plundered the Netherlands in the 9th and 10th centuries. On eight different occasions, for example, they destroyed the great trading centre in Dorestad (rebuilt in the 15th century, it is now known as Wijk bij Duurstede). The Vikings could not be kept at bay until town and coastal defences were strengthened in the 11th century.

A Fragmentation of Power

Between the 11th to the 14th centuries, the Netherlands consisted of numerous semi-independent principalities governed by the counts. The name 'Holland' dates from a deed of 1083. Over the years, the county of Holland was extended at the expense of its neighbours. Trade increased, towns grew and the lot of the peasants improved as marshlands were reclaimed and new farming methods were introduced. Water boards were established to maintain the dykes and sluices.

Burgundians and Habsburgs

The dukes of Burgundy gained control over parts of the Netherlands, Belgium, and eastern France. After coming to power in 1419, Philip the Good set up assemblies (known as 'states') consisting of representatives from the nobility, clergy and towns. In 1464, delegates from all the states met in Bruges (now in Belgium)—an event which can be considered a milestone on the road to freedom because it was the first meeting of what later became the States General, or Dutch parliament.

In the meantime, Burgundian lands prospered: Antwerp became the principal port, the cloth industry provided widespread employment, and great artists (Jan van Eyck and Hieronymus Bosch) flourished. When Charles the Bold died, the duchy of Burgundy reverted to France and the other lands passed to the princely German house of the Habsburgs.

Another step toward political freedom came in 1477, when the States General forced Mary of Burgundy to sign the Great Privilege, a constitutional document conferring far-reaching local powers. The States General was entitled to meet whenever they liked and Mary was not permitted to wage war without their approval.

The Spanish Netherlands

The Emperor Charles V (1500–1558) ruled over a vast empire which embraced the Burgundian lands, the Spanish kingdoms of Aragon and Castille (including Mexico, Peru and the Philippines) and the Austrian States. He strongly opposed the Reformation but in 1555 was forced to sign a peace treaty which confirmed the right of German princes to choose freely either the Protestant or the Catholic religion for their subjects.

In practice, this meant that the Netherlands would remain Catholic, but the Reformation was already so advanced that magistrates refused to convict heretics and the repressive efforts of the Habsburgs failed. Charles abdicated in 1555 in favour of his son Philip II, who became king of Spain and lord of the 17 provinces which made up the Netherlands at the time.

The Dutch Revolt

Philip fiercely opposed the growth of Protestantism and any decentralisation of his royal government, thus offending William of Orange and the other great nobles who encouraged these liberal trends. At the same time, the economy took a sharp downturn, which added to the growing political unrest. In 1566, hundreds of noblemen petitioned the regent of the Netherlands (Margaret of Parma, Philip's half-sister) asking that the anti-heresy laws of the Inquisition be changed. One of Margaret's ministers, however, dismissed the nobles as 'nothing but beggars'—an insult which led all those who opposed the Spanish government to proudly adopt the title of 'Beggars' (*geuzen* in Dutch).

Philip sent in troops to crush Dutch opposition to his autocratic rule. William of Orange and thousands of other patriots fled from the Netherlands. Some of these exiles, whose properties had been seized by Philip's forces, called themselves 'Sea Beggars' (*Watergeuzen*) and took to the North Sea to oppose the Spanish. In 1572, the Sea Beggars and their allies captured Den Briel, a small seaport town. This success marked the beginning of a widespread popular uprising against Spanish domination.

In 1579, representatives from the seven northern (and predominantly Protestant) provinces signed the Union of Utrecht, under which they agreed to unite against Spain, maintain their traditional rights and liberties, and allow freedom of religion. This agreement became the bedrock on which the freedom of the Dutch Republic was founded.

A Republic is Born and the Golden Age Begins

The States General assumed sovereign power in 1588, creating the Republic of the Seven United Provinces. Spain tried, but failed, to reconquer the northern Netherlands and under the terms of the Twelve Years' Truce of 1609, it gave de facto recognition to the republic as an independent state.

The 17th century is known as the Golden Age because it was a time of remarkable cultural and economic progress in the Netherlands. (*Painting, architecture, music and other arts will be mentioned in the section* Dutch Culture *on pages*

142–148, in Chapter 7: What To See and When To See It.) The very fine achievements in these cultural fields, however, were made possible by the fact that during the early decades of the 17th century, the two Dutch provinces of Holland and Zeeland became—with Amsterdam as their hub—the centre of Europe's trade with the rest of the world.

Grain, salt, wine, herring, textiles and spices were shipped to the Baltic states. Dealing in spices, Dutch merchants began the colonisation of what is now Indonesia. The Dutch East India Company (also known by its Dutch initials as the VOC) was founded in 1602 and given control of the Netherlands' lucrative trade with Asia via the Indian Ocean. For two centuries it was the biggest and most powerful trading organisation in the world. Until it was eclipsed in the 18th century by the British East India Company, the VOC earned great profits: at one point, dividends on its shares ran as high as 3,600 per cent.

As a result, shipbuilding and related industries (sail- and rope-making) flourished. By 1650, the Dutch had over 2,500 merchant ships and 2,000 fishing vessels. Sugar refining and cloth weaving provided additional profit and employment.

Expansion Abroad

Dutch maritime skills played a decisive role in the creation of a far-flung commercial and colonial empire during the 17th century.

In 1609, the English captain Henry Hudson sailed the Dutch East India Company ship Halve Maen ('Half Moon') on an exploratory mission along the east coast of North America. During this voyage, Hudson discovered Manhattan Island (New York), which was subsequently bought from the Native Americans in the 1620s by the Dutch governor Peter Minuet. This transaction, which also included other eastern portions of what is now New York State, involved payment with strings of sea shells known as *wampum* or *sewant*.

The Dutch West India Company, which traded with both Africa and the Americas, was founded in 1621. Nieuw Amsterdam (now New York) was settled in 1625. The Dutch

The Dutch East Indiaman, Amsterdam—a reminder of Dutch maritime history.

West India Company took over Curaçao in 1634 and a Dutch governor-general controlled the Antilles. Two years later, there was also a Dutch governor general in Brazil.

Malacca (in Malaysia) was captured from the Portuguese in 1641. The Dutch discovered Tasmania and New Zealand the next year and Australia in 1644, but did not settle in any of these lands. They founded Cape Colony (South Africa) in 1652 and finally, they occupied Ceylon (Sri Lanka) in 1658.

Dutch colonial possessions proved to be transitory, however, and today only the Netherlands Antilles (which consists of the islands of Aruba, Curaçao and Bonaire off Venezuela's coast and Saba, St Eustatius and southern St Martin in the Leeward Islands) still belong to the Netherlands.

Wars with England and France

Fearing the Netherlands' near-monopoly in seaborne trade in the 17th and 18th centuries, however, England tried to claim hegemony over the North Sea. The clash in the mercantile policies of these countries led to four Anglo-Dutch wars between 1652 and 1780.

In the process, Louis XIV of France attacked the Netherlands in 1672 and although the country remained intact under the Peace of Nijmegen, the French invaded again in 1795 and were more successful. Napoleon Bonaparte set up his brother Louis as King of Holland and by 1813, this kingdom had formally become part of the French Empire.

A Reunited Country and the Reduction of Royal Power

After Napoleon was defeated at Waterloo in 1815, Prince William I of Orange, the son of the last *Stadhouder* (head of state) of the Republic of the Seven United Provinces, became King of the Netherlands, uniting the 17 northern and southern provinces after a separation of over 200 years.

William is remembered as the 'merchant-king' because of the great economic progress which marked his reign. His political skills, however, were less pronounced. In 1830, the Brussels Revolution led to the independence of Belgium and in 1840, he abdicated after announcing his intention to marry a Roman Catholic countess.

A constitutional revision of 1848 had sharply curtailed royal power but a later king, William III, found it hard to accept these limitations. He clashed repeatedly with the parliament but in the end was soundly defeated and had to accept that henceforth Dutch rulers would only be the symbols of the unity of the Dutch people, rather than the bearers of any political power. Constitutional monarchy was here to stay.

Evolving into an Industrial Society

Between 1840 and the outbreak of World War I in 1914, the Netherlands gradually changed from an agricultural society to a modern market-driven economy with a fair degree of government involvement. Machines took over much of the heavy manual work but brought in their wake many of the negative aspects of the Industrial Revolution, including child labour. Protests against these abuses grew, however, and a bill introduced in parliament in 1874 led to a government investigation into the condition of workers in factories.

As a result of the problems of industrialisation and the controversies over religious education, political parties came into being around 1880. In 1887, the constitution was revised to extend the vote to more men. Women, however, could not vote until 1919.

Although at one point over 30 per cent of the labour force was out of work during the Great Depression of the 1930s, the abundant raw materials from the Dutch East Indies and the Netherlands' strong position in international trade led to the growth of big multinational corporations such as Royal Dutch Shell and Philips.

MODERN TIMES

Since the end of World War II in 1945, the Netherlands has experienced a great many changes. With growing prosperity has come an extensive social welfare network. 'Pillarisation', a unique way of organising Dutch social life, has gradually disappeared. The Netherlands has become a multiracial society. Protecting the environment is now a major concern of government and citizens alike.

World War II and its Aftermath

The Netherlands had been neutral during World War I and pacifist ideals remained very strong thereafter. But Germany invaded the Netherlands in 1940 and quickly overwhelmed the weak Dutch defences. Queen Wilhelmina and her government found refuge in England, where through Radio Orange broadcasts, she encouraged her people to resist the Germans.

In 1944, Allied armies landed in Normandy and began the liberation of Europe. But the northern part of the Netherlands still had to suffer through a winter of famine, when starving people were reduced to eating tulip bulbs, before the whole country was finally set free in 1945 and the huge task of reconstruction could begin.

Between 102,000–107,000 Jews were rounded up in the Netherlands and killed by the Nazis. One of these was a 13-year-old girl named Anne Frank, whose sensitive diary remains a masterpiece of this tragic era.

Although the Dutch now see Germans in a more positive light, during and after the war many Dutch citizens were strongly anti-German—a feeling which has persisted in varying degrees to this very day.

Bicycle Joke

Here is a classic Dutch joke: when a Dutchman sees a German, he says to himself "I want my bike back!" This refers to the fact that during the war, German soldiers often confiscated Dutch bicycles for their own use. In fact, more than 100,000 bicycles were confiscated in 1942 alone.

Far-reaching Changes

With the war's end, important domestic and international changes came thick and fast in the Netherlands. To list but a few of them: Queen Wilhelmina was succeeded by her daughter Juliana in 1948. The foundations for an ambitious social welfare network were laid as the Dutch economy made steady progress. The former colony of Indonesia became independent. In 1949, the Netherlands joined the North Atlantic Treaty Organisation (NATO) and in 1957, the Dutch were among the founders of the European Economic Community—now known as the European Union (EU).

Prosperity and Social Services

In the 1960s, the Dutch economy continued to grow rapidly, aided by the discovery of huge natural gas reserves in the north-eastern province of Groningen. These gas revenues helped finance a welfare state which, despite its well-publicised complexity and its many shortcomings, is still quite remarkable for the excellence, depth and breadth of its social services.

Although they put a very high value on these services and would not want to live without them, the Dutch themselves are quick to complain, however, that the welfare state as a whole is an impenetrable thicket of laws and regulations. You'll have to be a real expert to be able to make your way through it.

'Pillarisation' Fades Away and Youth Flourishes

General prosperity and wider educational opportunities also eroded the unique Dutch custom of 'pillarisation' (social compartmentalisation), which we will discuss in the next section. New and more broadly-based political parties appeared, such as the Christian Democratic Appeal which embraced all the major religious factions.

In the same era, the youth subculture which had first appeared in California in the early 1960s quickly spread to the Netherlands. By 1965, Amsterdam's Provo (from *provocation*) movement was taunting Dutch authorities and infuriating the complacent Dutch middle class. The 1968 student revolt in Paris encouraged Dutch students to put forward demands of their own. Universities in the Netherlands gradually adapted themselves to most student demands and student activism declined in the 1970s.

THE DECLINE OF PILLARISATION

For hundreds of years the Dutch had a unique way of organising their own society. Known as 'pillarisation' (*verzuiling*, i.e. social compartmentalisation), this was the practice of using religious or political affiliation as one of the basic 'pillars' of Dutch life. Much of Dutch life was organised around this pillarisation.

There were deep historical roots for this policy. After the Reformation and the establishment of Protestant churches in the 16th century, the northern part of the Netherlands inclined toward Protestantism (the Dutch Reformed Church was the major Protestant denomination) while the southern part of the country tended to remain Roman Catholic.

Designed to prevent religious discord, pillarisation strongly encouraged Catholics, Protestants, liberals and socialists to follow parallel but separate paths through life.

In practice, this meant that there were Catholic schools, universities, trade unions, sports and social clubs; Protestant schools, universities, trade unions, sports and social clubs; and separate media outlets (television, radio and press) for the followers of each of these major beliefs.

The Dutch government, for its part, took pains to make sure that both Catholics and Protestants were represented on official bodies. A Protestant solicitor from the north of the Netherlands, for example, might be appointed as the Public Prosecutor in Maastricht, a predominantly Catholic city in the south. In private life, however, some religious prejudice persisted: a Protestant homeowner might refuse even to consider selling his or her house to a Catholic.

But beginning in the 1960s, general prosperity and wider educational opportunities in the Netherlands gradually weakened the hold of organised religion on Dutch life. The growth of a secular society, a stronger national government and the waning of church influence, all combined to cut the main props out from under the traditional policy of pillarisation.

For centuries, pillarisation was the keystone in the arch of Dutch cultural life. Since the 1960s, however, there has been slow, peaceful but, nevertheless, remarkable social change: pillarisation has gone into a terminal decline. One proof of this great cultural shift is that young Dutch men and women now in their 20s will categorically deny that pillarisation still exists at all.

A Mixed Blessing?

Such an enormous sea-change in Dutch culture has had both good and bad effects. On the positive side of the ledger, the Dutch now have more personal freedom because they no longer need to rely exclusively on religiously or politically based organisations for their professional and social success.

At the same time, however, some Dutch commentators speculate that this loosening of social control may have contributed, if only indirectly, to an increase in personal anxiety, to greater vandalism and to more drug use by young people. Conceivably, they say, in the future it may also lead to more social isolation for older people, who will not have communal organisations to rely on for support

A MULTIRACIAL SOCIETY

Labour shortages prompted the Dutch to recruit large numbers of workers from foreign countries, including Turkey and Morocco, many of whom brought their families to the Netherlands in the 1970s and settled there permanently. Together with immigrants coming from Suriname and the Antilles in the 1980s and asylum seekers fleeing from upheavals in their native lands, these men, women and children have turned the Netherlands into a multiracial society.

Ethnic minorities—mostly people from non-industrialised countries outside Europe—and immigrants from Eastern Europe now make up about 10 per cent of the population of the Netherlands. Since these newcomers want to preserve their own culture, the task of fully assimilating them into Dutch culture has proved to be much more difficult than originally expected.

PROTECTING THE ENVIRONMENT

Queen Juliana was succeeded by her daughter Beatrix in 1980 and during the first 15 years of her reign, the Netherlands moved ahead on a wide variety of fronts. One of the most important of these was the growth of a strong environmental ethic—a commitment to protect the environment not only in the Netherlands itself but also abroad.

The Dutch work hard to protect the environment: a nature reserve in the central Netherlands.

Perhaps as an antidote to their very densely populated and highly developed society, the Dutch have always had a strong commitment to protecting the environment. A superb public transportation network (trains, trams and buses), highlighted by special low-cost tickets for commuters and students, has been created to wean people away from the use of city-choking automobiles.

Apartment dwellers seek a bit of 'country life' by growing their own vegetables in carefully tended allotment gardens. The government's own Forestry Commission (*Staatsbosbeheer*) carefully manages the forests and woodlands in its charge. These are open to the public and are studded with trails, picnic areas and bike paths. More than 344 nature reserves managed by the privately-funded Nature Conservation Society (*Vereniging tot Behoud van Natuurmonumenten*) protect habitats for birds and other wildlife. Most of these are open to the public too.

By the 1980s, however, the Netherlands was facing some very severe environmental problems. Its flat topography and low elevation encouraged the infiltration of salt water into farmlands. Big European rivers (the Rhine, Maas and Scheldt) carried toxic waste products through the country and deposited them in the North Sea. Industrialisation, high population densities and intensive land use in the Netherlands itself exacerbated almost all kinds of pollution.

There was also a uniquely Dutch problem: disposing of all the manure produced each day by the country's five million cows and 14 million pigs—only a small portion of which could be used as fertiliser for farms.

These problems still persist but good progress is being made in dealing with them. The Dutch public and the Dutch government are deadly serious about cleaning up the environment and are demanding costly remedial efforts by industries and private citizens alike.

Dutch industries have drawn up more than 75 voluntary covenants with the government to reduce pollution and conserve energy. An 'Environmental Technology Valley' has been established in Apeldoorn to attract companies making innovations in environmental technology. Households are producing less waste and separate garbage containers enable the waste to be collected and processed more efficiently. Commuters are encouraged to use bicycles, trains and buses rather than cars. Farmers are induced to cut back on the use of pesticides and artificial fertilisers.

In essence, a new balance is being struck between economic development on the one hand and the conservation of nature on the other. A successful compromise along these lines was the Eastern Scheldt Dam, completed in 1986. If necessary, the gates of the dam can be closed at high water levels to prevent floods. The daily tidal flows, however, are not affected, thus assuring that the Eastern Scheldt remains a biologically productive waterway—and this was what the environmentalists and oyster farmers were after.

International Cooperation

Abroad, the Netherlands continues to play a very active role in international efforts to protect the global environment. For many years, to take just one example, the Dutch have worked closely with other countries along the Rhine and with Belgium to reduce transborder river pollution. Together with 140 other countries, the Netherlands has signed the Kyoto Protocol, which aims to reduce emissions of greenhouse gases. By the year 2012, the Netherlands hopes to have reduced its own emissions by 6 per cent.

THE DUTCH PEOPLE

'From the comfort of their immaculate sitting rooms the Dutch may acknowledge that they are the cleanest people on earth, are thrifty, have a canny head for business, an unparalleled facility with languages, an unequalled ability to get along with one another and with foreigners, and an inimitable charm. But they will be far too modest, unless pushed, to admit publicly that all this makes them somewhat superior to other nations.'
—Rodney Bolt, *The Xenophobe's Guide to the Dutch*

HOW DO THE DUTCH SEE THEMSELVES?

By drawing on some of the points made by the Royal Tropical Institute in Amsterdam when it teaches foreigners about life in the Netherlands and which are echoed by Han van der Horst in his excellent book *The Low Sky*, one can say that the well-educated Dutch like to imagine themselves as—and certainly hope that foreigners will see them as—an egalitarian, practical, well-organised people who value privacy and self-control, who are thrifty and drive a hard bargain, and who are experts in international trade.

The Dutch are Not Perfect

To some extent, of course, this very flattering self-image is only a myth. In reality, the Dutch are certainly not angels. Their proverbial bluntness is not to everyone's taste. Many of them are neither intelligent, well-educated, tolerant, considerate, prosperous, multilingual, friendly towards foreigners nor low-key and quiet. Some of them, in fact, especially the hooligans at football (soccer) matches, fall far short of the idealised national standards. Indeed, in 1997, one person died as a result of injuries sustained at a fight between football supporters of two rival clubs.

Another shortcoming may be that the Dutch are so committed to equality, compromise and avoiding conflict that they have created a labyrinth of rules and regulations from which there is no easy exit. Mastering all these, sometimes conflicting, legal and procedural requirements is hard enough for the Dutch themselves. And foreigners trying to make their way through this Kafkaesque maze may well begin to despair if they hear too often from Dutch bureaucrats the blunt statement, "That's not possible!"

What we are saying here is that the Netherlands is not, in fact, an earthly paradise. Despite your very best efforts, you may find that you simply cannot get along with some Dutch people. Nevertheless, the positive traits listed above are the ones set by the upper middle class and the ones which most Dutch try to teach their children at home and at school. So let us look briefly at each of these idealised national characteristics in turn.

The Dutch are Egalitarian

The rich/poor gap which is so painfully visible in Britain, the US and in many other developed countries simply does not exist to the same extent in the Netherlands, which prides itself on being a truly egalitarian society. Indeed, since the end of World War II, the Dutch have virtually eliminated life-threatening poverty in their own country. Thanks to a healthy economy, the unemployment rate—now only about 3.2 per cent—is the lowest in the European Union.

Officially, only a small percentage of the inhabitants in the four largest cities—mainly the single 45- to 64-year-olds, one-parent families, and couples with many underage children—fall below the poverty line, which is set relatively high. This figure is deceptive, however, because the most likely reason these people are officially classified as 'poor' is that, for one reason or another, they are not using all the unemployment, housing and other social benefits to which they are fully entitled. In fact, it is estimated that only about 2 per cent of all Dutch households are in serious financial trouble.

One reason for this is that it is very difficult for a person to fall through the tightly-woven safety net provided by the Dutch welfare system. Unless you are, say, a drug addict or a mentally ill person with no fixed address and who categorically refuses to ask for help, the government will give you various kinds of assistance and enough money to ensure your survival, albeit at a very modest level.

At the same time, however, it is equally difficult in the Netherlands to rise to the very top of the business world or any of the professions. Stiff and progressively higher taxes are only part of the problem. The real issue is that just as they do not like to see some people falling by the wayside, the Dutch do not like to see others rising too high: they really do practise social equality.

One proof of this is that there are comparatively few millionaires in the country—just over 100,000, according to one recent count.

Perhaps a reflection of this fact is found in a classic Dutch saying: *Doe maar gewoon, dan doe je al gek genoeg* or 'behave normally, that's mad enough'. The Dutch commitment to normality reflects a conviction that in such a small, densely-populated country, assertive, aggressive or flamboyant behaviour is inherently unequal. It is also likely to offend other people.

By the same token, riches should not be flaunted. Well-heeled individuals should not throw money around or treat themselves to lavish houses, expensive parties or flashy cars. And unlike the British monarchy, the House of Orange (the Dutch royal family)—aided, to be sure, by the Netherlands' rigorous privacy laws which keep the media at arms' length—maintains a low public profile, avoids scandals and shuns extravagances.

It is not surprising then, that tolerance, moderation and respect for others are the three cardinal virtues for the well-educated Dutch. These Golden Rules not only encourage social equality in the society as a whole but also help ensure that the individual can pursue his or her own interests without any interference. The individual is considered to be the best judge of his or her destiny. A Dutch motto along these lines is *Laat iedereen in zijn waarde*, or 'to each his own'.

At the same time, the Dutch want equality for other people too, both those who live in the Netherlands itself and those who are sunk into Third World poverty or who find themselves in the war zones.

Caring for the Less Fortunate

Simon Schama, the British historian who wrote the magisterial book *The Embarrassment of Riches*, begins it with a quote from John Calvin, the puritanical theologian who was one of the leaders of the Protestant Reformation: "Let those who have abundance remember that they are surrounded with thorns, and let them take great care not to be pricked by them." Calvin apparently feared that prosperous Dutch citizens would become so morally tainted by their own wealth that they would selfishly refuse to care for the needy.

Perhaps it is with Calvin's stern warning embedded in their subconscious that the educated Dutch of today are so willing to help the less fortunate. There is an extensive social welfare system at home and widespread public support for generous foreign aid and for international peacekeeping operations abroad. Calvin would certainly approve: he would have no trouble defending these activities—chiefly on moral grounds, to be sure, but perhaps also as a practical way to keep the have-nots from becoming a threat to those who have a comfortable abundance.

The Dutch are Practical

Most of the Dutch are less concerned with metaphysical questions than with finding practical solutions to immediate problems, the chief of which has always been the war against the water. In this endless battle, the Dutch, armed first with windmills and later with pumping stations, have been largely successful—'God made the world,' runs the old saying, 'but the Dutch made the Netherlands'.

Eternal vigilance, however, is the price of this victory. The Dutch will literally never be able to drop their guard. Every day, the 1,931 km (1,200 miles) of dykes, dams and dunes must be kept in good repair; every day, water that percolates into the polders must be drained and pumped out. No one has described the need for this vigilance better than the poet Hendrik Marsman (1899–1940). In his poem *Herinnering aan Holland* (*Memories of Holland*), written in 1936–1937, he tells us:

en in alle gewesten	And in every region
wordt de stem van het water	The voice of the water
met zijn eeuwige rampen	Telling of endless disaster
gevreesd en gehoord	Is heard and feared.

These prophetic words were borne out in 1953, when a very high tide driven by a very strong wind flooded 259,889 hectares (642,200 acres) of the Netherlands, killing 1,865 people, making hundreds of thousands of others homeless, and drowning more than a million cattle. The Dutch response—practicality here on a truly vast scale—was to build a network of huge dams (the Delta Works) to protect the south-western coast and its inland areas.

Perhaps it is this practical, no-nonsense approach to water management which gives the Dutch some of their less adorable characteristics. To be sure, they can be helpful and friendly but they can also be painfully direct, outspoken, stubborn and blunt—as implied by the term 'Dutch uncle', a well-meaning but, when the occasion calls for it, an unrelenting critic.

In *The Embarrassment of Riches*, Simon Schama gives a 17th century example of Dutch straightforwardness. When the Dutch presented to Henry, Prince of Wales, a massive gold casket full of valuable annuity bonds, an English courtier tried to downplay the value of the present by dismissing it with the laconic sigh of '*puf*'. The Dutch emissary quickly

A high standard of living and an egalitarian ideal characterise Dutch society.

corrected him: "*Non puf est*," he said in blunt Latin, "*sed aurum purum*." ('This is not *puf*, but pure gold!')

Dutch self-assurance has continued down the years. Trying to explain the Dutch mentality to the US troops serving in the Netherlands during World War II, the American anthropologist Margaret Mead joked that "the Dutch are always right." Then, with tongue firmly in cheek, she added, "in this they resemble the Americans."

If some of the Dutch are very practical and think they are always right, it follows that they should also be good debaters. And indeed many of them are. These men and women are willing to offer their own opinions on any subject under discussion. "*Ja, maar...*" (yes, but...) is a common interjection whenever one speaker pauses for breath, however briefly, during a conversation.

And since they think they know how matters really should be arranged, some of the Dutch are also prone to grumble about the perceived injustices—personal, social, academic, job-related, national or international—which are allegedly being inflicted upon them every day. Even here, however, many Dutch manage to keep a sense of humour and do not take themselves too seriously. An elderly Dutchman remembered that when he was growing up his father always told him, "Skip the complaints!"

The Dutch are Well-organised

Because they like to lead busy lives, being on time is usually very important to the Dutch. Making—and keeping—appointments is no less important to them; to make sure they do, diaries are in frequent use, especially when the vitally important issue of *overleg* is involved.

Overleg: The Search for Common Ground

Overleg has no exact equivalent in English. A literal translation would be 'to consult together' but the British phrase 'in conference' is more to the point.

Overleg is a slow, consensus-building exercise in which everyone at a meeting has the opportunity to participate. Teamwork is important here. The goal is not to rubber-stamp the chairperson's own preference but to exchange information and to hammer out a workable compromise which all the participants can endorse. In the office, meetings can drag on endlessly because so much importance is attached to the right to express one's personal opinion in full detail. The impression that something was actually *settled* at a meeting may well prove to be incorrect later on. Some participants may insist: "We didn't *agree* to anything. We only discussed it!" A Dutch maxim captures this line of thought very nicely: 'It is better to debate a question without settling it than to settle it without debating it.'

Reaching a decision by this process can be time-consuming, but the Dutch believe that things move faster in the long run if the chairperson can announce with pleasure, *de klokken zijn gelijk gezet* ('the clocks are all showing the same time'), or we are all agreed on the solution.

One thing that really keeps even the non-religious Dutch on their toes is the Calvinist doctrine of hard work. A job must be done on time but equally importantly, it must also be done well. Shoddy work or corruption is not tolerated. Individuals or companies which do not maintain high standards will soon be out of business.

This is the reason visitors to the Netherlands are invariably impressed by the very high quality of Dutch products and by the visible pride which even small tradespeople (butchers, fishmongers, florists and cobblers) take in doing their jobs well. Perhaps this is because the non-religious Dutch of today are still aware of the traditional clergyman's *vermanende vinger* (wagging finger), warning them of the moral dangers of idleness and slovenly work.

The Dutch Value Privacy and Self-control

Although they may not be as restrained and as polite as the British, the Dutch usually respect other people's privacy and would be the first to agree that a man's home is his castle. But the neighbours' home is their castle too, and adults are supposed to exercise some self-control. To be sure, as we have indicated, not all Dutch are quiet, sober citizens, and not all of them dislike gossip. But while it may be honoured in

The Calvinist attitude to hard work is so strong among the Dutch that even the small tradespeople, such as this shoeshine man, take a lot of pride in what they do.

the breach, the cultural ideal is nevertheless to be considerate and not to cause commotion.

Gezelligheid: The Pursuit of Cosiness

Within their immaculately clean homes (proudly exposed to public view because the curtains are rarely drawn), the Dutch can revel in *gezelligheid*, a national trait which defies easy translation into English. According to the dictionary, *gezellig* means 'cosy' but it really implies much more, namely, family or friends being all together, with everyone being happy and in a good mood. A mother, for example, will call out 'keep it *gezellig*!' when her children become too rowdy.

The Dutch are Thrifty and Strike a Hard Bargain

Despite their wealth, the Dutch have a long reputation as penny-pinchers. In his famous 18th century satire, for example, the French writer Voltaire tells us, tongue-in-cheek, that after his fictional hero Candide had been robbed in Suriname by a Dutch merchant, Candide complained, loudly and at length, to a Dutch judge. The judge patiently agreed to look into the matter when the merchant returned but in the meantime charged Candide 10,000 piasters for making too much noise and an additional 10,000 piasters for the hearing itself!

The Dutch are Experts in International Trade

Long before the Dutch East India Company was founded in 1602, Dutch seamen and merchants were deeply involved in international trade. Their descendants are now at the forefront of the current drive toward globalisation—treating the whole world as a single unified market for goods, services and ideas.

Not for nothing is the Netherlands known as 'the gateway to Europe'. Nearly 5,200 km (3,000 miles) of navigable inland waterways link the Netherlands to neighbouring Belgium, France and Germany. Forty per cent of the road transport in Europe is handled by the Dutch. Schiphol, the Netherlands' main airport, has about 89 airlines serving 219 destinations and handles more than 46 million passengers a year.

Rotterdam, strategically located at the mouth of the Rhine and the Maas rivers, is a key trans-shipment point for foreign goods coming into northern Europe. Indeed, in terms of the tonnage handled, this is the busiest port in the world, where over 35,000 seagoing ships bring in nearly 377 million metric tonnes of cargo each year. A good part of this cargo is off-loaded onto smaller vessels which deliver goods to German buyers via the Rhine.

In 2007, the Betuweroute, a dedicated double-track freight railway linking Rotterdam and Germany, went into operation. It can handle up to 480 freight trains per day.

A SUMMING UP

Even if you have never lived abroad before, you will probably find that living and working in the Netherlands is not that difficult. The Dutch are not angels, but to get along with most of them, all you really have to do, in a nutshell, is to follow the advice offered by a young Dutch couple: "Be yourself," they said, "and respect other people."

THE CYCLE OF LIFE IN THE NETHERLANDS

The universal cycle of life—childhood, student days, marriage, middle age, retirement, old age, and death—in the Netherlands often has a special 'Dutch touch', which adds a few differences to these familiar human milestones. Knowing something about this will make it easier for you to understand Dutch society and adjust to it. Yet even if Dutch women are the oldest first-time mothers in Europe, they are not particularly career-minded either. Part-time work is still hugely popular.

NON-WORKING MOTHERS

Compared to the USA, the UK and many other developed countries, there are still relatively few mothers working full-time in the Netherlands. In fact, only 25 per cent of Dutch women think that having children and a career can be successfully combined.

There seem to be four reasons behind the large number of stay-at-home mothers:

- Certainly the most important is the very strong Dutch tradition of a familial society—a society where family life is extremely important and where the mother's constant presence in the house is seen as essential for the proper upbringing of the children.
- Homemakers themselves have always been highly valued. In the past, working mothers were accepted but not necessarily praised; indeed, they might even have been quietly criticised for being 'over-ambitious'. Self-esteem is not a problem here; non-working mothers today are every bit as self-confident as women who work.
- Dutch schoolchildren almost always come home for lunch, which the mother herself has to prepare. Children also come home from school at 3:30 pm or even earlier. The Netherlands lags far behind many other countries in providing childcare facilities for 3–4-year-olds; a nanny or other kind of childcare is costly and hard to find.
- There is sometimes no economic necessity for a woman to work because her husband's income may be adequate for family needs.

A Dutch mother and son. A 'gezellig' moment. A vast majority of Dutch mothers are the stay-at-home variety as many believe that the constant presence of the mother is essential to the proper upbringing of children.

So, until very recently, it was expected as a matter of course that even well-educated, highly-trained young women would stop working when their first child was born and would not go back to full-time work until after the last child had left the nest. If they worked outside the home before then, it would only be at part-time jobs. Even today, 75 per cent of the Dutch women who have children and who are also working are holding down part-time jobs.

Some Consequences

Taking such a long break from full-time work in order to raise children means that Dutch women tend to fall behind their men in terms of work experience and the technical knowledge which can only be picked up on the job. This gender disparity has often resulted in women earning less than men.

Another problem now considerably eased by the recent economic boom and consequent labour shortage, was the difficulty unemployed women faced in finding full-time jobs once they exceeded the age of 40. So after the last child, many middle-aged women have not even bothered to look for full-time work. This has left volunteer work, part-time jobs or courses at local universities as their usual alternatives.

MORE WORKING WOMEN

Dutch culture is changing on the labour front because there is a rapid increase in the total number of working women. In 1981, only 30 per cent of women were working outside the home. By 2005, 68 per cent of Dutch women had a part-time job of between 12 and 34 hours per week. Half of the working mothers with children would now like to work even more, provided that they can fit a longer working week into their family lives. The number of working women is expected to rise further in the years ahead. The key reason for these impressive changes is that home-owning has become the middle class norm in the Netherlands. As in many other developed countries, house prices have risen steeply. For most Dutch couples, home-ownership is almost impossible on only one income.

CHILDHOOD
Raising Children

Before World War II, big families (ten or more children) were not uncommon in the predominately Catholic southern part of the Netherlands. Since birth control was not widespread then, workers and rural folk of modest means often found themselves with very large families.

But times change and having two to three children is now the norm. Birth control is practised universally. Some couples do not marry because they think marriage is unnecessary, old-fashioned or too restrictive, but they decide to have children nevertheless. According to a 2007 United Nations International Children's Emergency Fund (UNICEF) report, children in the Netherlands now have the best quality of life of all the 21 industrialised countries in the Organization for Economic Cooperation and Development (OECD). The Netherlands topped the list; Sweden, Denmark and Finland claimed, respectively, the next three places; the US and the UK ranked at the bottom.

No Brat Pack

Dutch children are raised very permissively rather than strictly. There are no gender differences here: boys and girls are brought up the same way because their parents think all human beings should be treated equally.

Parents expect that their children will be heard as well as seen and will have their say in family decisions. Most parents feel that children should have the freedom, within some loose limits, to say and do just what they please. This belief is echoed by TV programmes for children, which often poke fun at parents' relative conservatism and at society's many rules and regulations.

Strangely enough, such extreme permissiveness usually does not, in the long run, produce spoiled, bratty children. Most middle-class parents (i.e. the vast majority of the population) do try, consciously or unconsciously, to conform to those 'ideal' traits of the Dutch character that we discussed earlier in this chapter. In so doing they set an example, which the children are quick to perceive

A Dutch father spends some quality time with his baby.

as constituting 'good' behaviour and for which they will eventually be praised.

Behaviour, Good and Bad

What constitutes 'good' behaviour for a Dutch child? Some examples: children are warmly praised for being polite, honest, straightforward, doing well at sports and getting passing if not top grades at school. They are mildly reproved for 'bad' behaviour: not being able to amuse themselves, interrupting adult conversations to get attention, doing poorly at school, bullying other children or stealing.

The net result is that most of these free-spirited children will end up following the lead of their parents and will gradually evolve into hard-working, responsible, tolerant and well-mannered young adults, not barbarians or dropouts.

Teenagers

It is worth mentioning too, that while the Dutch do have a few problems with their teenagers, there is really not much of a generation gap in the Netherlands. As a result, teenage problems do not seem to be as overwhelming (for young people and parents alike) as they are in some other countries.

Indeed, Dutch teenagers seem to be a fairly conservative lot. Opinion surveys indicated that while only 30 per cent of the 18-year-olds interviewed think that a steady relationship is necessary before people have sexual intercourse, fully 50 per cent of them are still virgins at that age.

Freedom to Choose

Dutch parents are very tolerant. They do not expect that their children will necessarily follow in parental footsteps and do not put any real pressure on them to do so. Parents may try to steer children in one general direction or another, but young people are expected to orient themselves and are free to choose whatever professions or lifestyles they like. Well-educated parents, however, do hope that their children will look for jobs which involve a relatively high intellectual level of work.

Adoption

Because of widespread birth control, few unwanted children are born in the Netherlands, so very few are available for adoption. If a suitable child can be found, the adoption process itself will take a long time (two to ten years) because of the careful background checks designed to prevent child abuse. There is no social or legal discrimination against adopted children.

Student Days

The Dutch education system is one of the best and most extensive in the world today. It is strict, formally organised and gives students exposure to different subjects. Knowing something about it can help you understand why the overall quality of life in the Netherlands is remarkably high.

It is so high simply because most Dutch men and women are quite competent professionally. This is not to say that they are more intelligent than other people in the world but that in most cases, they know their jobs well and do them well. The underlying reason for this happy state of affairs is probably that they have been trained very well at school.

Indeed, compared to their counterparts in the US or UK, Dutch students do not have the luxury of simply drifting through school. They have to work very hard: most secondary school students must do two to three hours of homework every day. High standards mean that degrees are not obtained easily: the average graduate course lasts more than five years.

The Netherlands will face several educational challenges in the coming years. The most important of these are the need to make further improvements in the quality of education and to provide equal opportunities for everyone, a variety of choices in education, and specially tailored content and counseling for students who need it. The greatest threat to the Dutch education system is the increasing shortage of teachers, which is due in part to relatively low pay in comparison with other professions.

THE DUTCH EDUCATION SYSTEM: AN OVERVIEW

This education system consists of
- primary schools
- secondary schools, of which there are several kinds
- vocational schools
- special schools
- institutes of higher learning
- institutes of international education
- adult education schools

Dutch Education System

By far the best way to learn about the complicated details of the Dutch education system is through the Internet—specifically via the website:

http://www.overheid.nl

which is the central access point to all information about government organisations in the Netherlands, including those on tourism, trade and culture. To access the pages in English, click on 'English'.

Primary Schools

Primary schools are designed for children between the ages of four and 12. At first (during the first three years of primary school), the main emphasis is on the child's development. At the same time, a learn-by-playing curriculum introduces children to reading, writing and arithmetic. They also learn some elementary social and manual skills.

In the next five years, they are taught Dutch, mathematics, history, geography, environmental awareness and social science. All schools also teach art and have facilities for physical exercise. English is sometimes taught, beginning in the last year of primary school. This is the reason so many Dutch speak (but not necessarily write) English so well: they begin studying it at the age of 12.

Secondary Schools

Secondary education, which begins at the age of 12 with a period of basic secondary education, includes four different kinds of schools. These offer, respectively:

- pre-university education (known by its Dutch initials as VWO; 6 years, ages 12–18)
- senior general secondary education (HAVO; 5 years, ages 12–17)
- pre-vocational secondary education (VMBO; 4 years, ages 12–16)
- Practical Training (PRO; ages 12–18).

Vocational Education

In vocational education, courses of study are adjusted to suit the labour market. There is a growing demand for graduates of upper secondary vocational education (MBO) and for those of higher professional education (HBO). Thus an important goal of the Netherlands' education system is now to encourage students to move on to higher secondary school levels and not to drop out.

Special Schools

These teach mentally handicapped, physically disabled or maladjusted children, or children with learning disabilities.

What Happens to School Dropouts?

Not all Dutch students do brilliantly. They may be unruly and impatient or lack motivation. If, in addition, to these behaviour and attitude problems, a student comes from a family with low educational levels, he or she has greater likelihood of becoming a dropout.

In some developed countries, students who do poorly and drop out of secondary school are likely to end up unemployed (perhaps permanently) and may well turn to drugs or crime. Things are different in the Netherlands.

In the first place, students are simply not permitted to leave secondary school before the age of 16. If they do poorly at one school, they are transferred to a lower-level school and are given special attention. Work-study programmes are also strongly encouraged.

Ultimately, however, it is the safety net provided by the Dutch welfare system that keeps teenage school-leavers from utter destitution and helps to reduce the appeal of drugs and crime.

In recent years, for example, an unmarried unemployed person under the age of 21 has been eligible for about 204 euros per month in 'income support' plus an additional holiday allowance of about 10 euros per month. A young person could not live on this total alone but if he or she also took advantage of all the other social benefits which are available, there would be no need to starve, sleep in the street or turn to drugs and crime.

So Dutch dropouts usually do not fail: in fact, 66 per cent of them end up finding some kind of paid employment or go into some other field of education. The downside is that they often become flexi-workers and are faced with temporary jobs with reduced prospects of advancement.

Institutes of Higher Education

The average level of education in the Netherlands has been rising sharply. Whereas only 15 per cent of men over 65 have a higher education, 27 per cent of younger men between the ages of 25–44 have qualifications. The increase in women's education has been even more striking. For those over 65, only 6 per cent went beyond secondary school; but 22 per cent of younger women aged 22–44 have a higher education.

The race for educational qualification continues because, in the Netherlands today, a good education is the keystone to career success. People therefore want more and more certificates of higher education.

This is posing a financial problem to the Dutch government, which is trying to contain this stream of people by cutting education costs and by limiting the time students have to finish their studies. Schools feel the financial pinch too, and are faced with having to make hard choices between the quality and quantity of education they offer.

Higher education studies begin at the age of 18. There are 18 universities in the Netherlands (including the Open University, which offers correspondence courses) as well as numerous colleges for higher professional education. Leiden University, founded in 1575 by Prince William of Orange, is the oldest university in the Netherlands. Wageningen University (formerly known as the Landbouwhogeschool) is the leading European university in the life sciences. Specialising in plant and animal food and food production, it attracts students from more than 100 countries.

The Dutch universities and colleges of higher education are financed by the state. In addition, there are seven theological colleges which are financed partly from government funds. Higher education, however, is not free.

The Dutch government gives students a stipend but this is not enough to cover all their expenses. The stipend is only about 230 euros per month (about 2,760 euros per year), whereas the total cost of university education is more than 6,800 euros per year.

To make ends meet, university students must therefore ask for parental support, borrow money at low interest rates, or get part-time jobs. Most of them prefer to find jobs than be a burden on their parents or go into debt. In 1996, however, a 'results grant' was introduced. This means that students in higher education can begin by borrowing money. If their grades are good, these loans will become a grant or at least a partial grant.

University courses are given in two stages. The first lasts from four to six years and concludes with the *doctoraal* examination—hence the title 'Drs' (*doctorandus*) which you will often see on Dutch business cards. The second stage, designed for relatively few students who wish to become scholars or professors, involves highly specialised courses of study or research leading to a doctorate (PhD).

A country of rich hues: Netherlands is known for its beautiful and vibrant flowers, which can be bought at the various markets.

Most homes in the the cities are pleasant and cosy. Apartments are usually located above little shops and cafes and street signs are clear and easy to follow.

A view of St. Nicholas Church in Amsterdam. Although there is religious diversity in the country, there has been a decline of religious adherence and the church is likewise on a decline.

Visitors at the Rijksmuseum are mesmerised by the works of art on display.

The interior of Magna Plaza in Amsterdam. This grand building used to be the former Head Post Office, but is now a posh shopping centre featuring many international brands.

Institutes of International Education

Expatriates living and working in the Netherlands have a wide choice of schools for their children. Options for international education include:

- boarding schools, some coeducational
- British, American, French and German schools
- Dutch schools with a special English-language stream, e.g. for an International Baccalaureate
- regular Dutch schools

An informative folder, published by the Foundation for International Education (Stichting Internationaal Onderwijs), gives many useful details. Visit their Internet site at:

http://www.sio.nl

Adult Education

Adult education is becoming increasingly popular in the Netherlands and it is estimated that 37 per cent of Dutch adults are enrolled in an educational course of some kind. Men tend to focus on practical, career-oriented subjects; women are more inclined to take courses on cultural subjects.

In addition to the Open University mentioned above, there are Adult Education Centres (Volksuniversiteit). You can also check with a local university to see if it offers part-time studies in English, for example, in the evening or during the day.

MARRIAGE
Weddings

Young men and women meet each other in their own social circles and at schools, clubs and bars. Statistically, the average age of getting married is 31.5 years.

Most people will live together for a few years (with full parental blessing) before deciding to get married. Fifty-five per cent of women under the age of 27 have lived with a partner and usually decide to get married when they expect a baby.

When couples do get married, there are often two separate ceremonies. The first is always a civil ceremony at the Town Hall. Legally, this is the only wedding that counts because it alone forges the bonds of marriage. But some people want a church wedding as well. However, a church ceremony is, so to speak, only frosting on the cake: the man and woman were already legally married at the Town Hall.

After the ceremony, there is usually a reception for many guests, followed by a smaller gathering for the couple's family and closest friends.

Knowing Who Your Friends Are

Here the bride and groom (and perhaps their parents, too) must make very difficult social decisions as they plan these events. Dutch custom requires that the invitations sent to all the guests must state if they are invited to the smaller party. Those who are not invited may be unhappy. As one foreign resident of Amsterdam explains, "People who thought themselves close friends may be lost for life if they come down on the wrong side of the great divide."

Contracts

A formal 'contract of living together', also known as a registered partnership, is commonly drawn up by couples who live together but do not want to get married immediately or, indeed, at all. Most Dutch couples get married only after having lived together for some time.

Divorce

The Dutch are conservative about marriage, usually staying faithful to their partner and sometimes believing that a bad marriage is better than none at all.

Nevertheless, roughly 33 per cent of all Dutch marriages will end in divorce, a figure which has remained remarkably consistent over the last 20 years. Divorces in the Netherlands are socially acceptable, relatively easy to get and, depending on the amount of money at stake and how long the squabbles go on, comparatively cheap. Children from the age of 12 have a say in which parent they would like to live with. There are also a few 'divorces of convenience' purely for tax reasons.

If they do have a troubled marriage, the Dutch do not turn instinctively to marriage counselling sessions or to other forms of therapy. These aids certainly exist but are not thought to do much good, at least in terms of saving the marriage itself.

MIDDLE AGE
In the Netherlands today, as is the case in the US and UK, more and more middle-aged/middle management employees in their late forties and early fifties are being declared redundant or are being forced into early retirement.

This is because the traditional pyramid structures of Dutch organisations are changing due to cost-cutting measures and to the information revolution ushered in by ever-faster computers. Nowadays there is no need for so many expensive, older white-collar employees. As a result, job uncertainty and job-hopping have increased among them as the younger generation begins to take over.

The result is that only 52 per cent of the men and 27 per cent of the women between the ages of 55 and 64 are still on the job. Those who have left the full-time workforce do not usually get a lucrative 'golden handshake'. A Dutch banker joked that "they may get a handshake of some kind, but it won't be golden!"

Once out of the office, however, they will find that, thanks to labour shortages, getting a temporary job is relatively easy. Moreover, some people have saved to finance an early retirement. Thus, one way or another, retired people manage to make ends meet.

RETIREMENT
The official retirement age is 65 but most men stop working at the age of 61 and most women at the age of 60. Both private employers and the Dutch government provide retirement benefits. People in the private sector claim that Dutch civil servants fare very well indeed and that their benefits are among the best in the world.

OLD AGE, EUTHANASIA AND DEATH
Older parents do not live with their children. They first try to live on their own for as long as possible. Eventually, they may

The official retirement age is 65 but many people in their sixties opt to retire early. Many are independent, living on their own and caring for themselves until they are too infirmed and have to be admitted into a nursing home.

move into a serviced flat, where one hot meal is provided each day. Later on, when they need more care, they may move into a retirement home and, ultimately, into a nursing home. Government welfare payments and a small old age pension after 65 contribute to their financial support.

Euthanasia

When a patient is suffering unbearable pain and has no prospects of improvement, euthanasia is legal in the Netherlands, provided that carefully-scripted guidelines are followed. The number of euthanasia cases in the Netherlands fell sharply in the four years since the introduction of new legislation in 2002. In 2005, there were about 2,300 cases of euthanasia. At the same time, cases of 'palliative sedation' rose 11 per cent. Palliative sedation involves administering a sedative to a patient who is expected to die within two weeks. Its purpose is to make death painless.

Death

When death occurs, the Dutch do not arrange lavish funerals or engage in public displays of mourning, preferring instead to keep their feelings to themselves or within the family circle.

There will be a church service or a secular gathering at the *Uitvaartcentrum* (departure centre), either of which will be followed by a reception where coffee and cake are served. Subdued colours are worn—but not necessarily black, because this might be overdoing it. There are now slightly more cremations than burials.

DUTCH SOCIETY

CHAPTER 4

'Huil niet, wordt niet onwaardig boos. Begrip.'
('Do not weep; do not wax indignant. Understand.')
—Dutch-Jewish philosopher Baruch Spinoza

A GENTLE SOCIETY:
THE NETHERLANDS TODAY

What can we say about the Netherlands today—about the quality of life, social welfare, the economy, trade unions, domestic politics, military forces, Water Control Boards, foreign policies and, last but not least, about drugs and crime?

THE QUALITY OF LIFE IS VERY HIGH

One of the things that may strike you after you have lived in the Netherlands for a few months is that the overall quality of life is extraordinarily high.

Although they never tire of complaining that standards have slipped in recent years, most of the Dutch will, when pressed, agree that the quality of life in the Netherlands is still very high. They would probably attribute this to a number of interrelated factors: general prosperity, social quality, good health care, a good education system, racial and religious tolerance, little political extremism, little poverty, relatively little violent crime and (thanks to the many rules and regulations) a workable balance between the needs of the individual and the needs of society as a whole.

Allied to all this is, one can add, a long tradition of hard, competent work. Other countries may also have a saying along the lines of 'work before pleasure' but the Dutch give this adage a more humorous and more explicit twist:

werk gaat voor het meisje, they say, 'Work comes before the girlfriend!'

GOOD MARKS FROM FOREIGN BUSINESSMEN AND OFFICIALS

This exceptionally high quality of life allows foreign businessmen to give the Netherlands good marks in all of the areas they consider to be priorities for employees being assigned here: accommodation, personal security, schooling for children, leisure facilities, environment (clean air and water) and cultural and social facilities.

Human Progress

In fact, according to a United Nations (UN) Human Development Report, which measured human progress by linking economic growth to social factors rather than looking at economic growth alone, the Netherlands is the best country to live in within the European Union and the fourth-best globally (after Canada, the US and Japan). A compelling case can be made, however, for the proposition that for the average man or woman in the street, the overall quality of life in the Netherlands is actually much higher than it is in the US or Canada.

Dutch life expectancy at birth—about 77 years for men and almost 82 years for women—is quite high and thanks to high enrolment rates in primary, secondary and tertiary schools. The Netherlands also scores well in educational achievement. Income distribution is above-average compared to other highly developed countries. Although the rate of violent urban crime has risen in the Netherlands, it is still low when compared with other developed countries (notably the US).

Some Shortcomings

But the Netherlands does not merit a straight-A report card. According to a survey by an Internet magazine on international living, the Netherlands is the third most pleasant country to live in (after France and Australia). The criteria used in this survey included cost of living, tax levels, climate, opportunities for expanding markets, safety and environmental pollution. The Netherlands scored high in most categories but did particularly well in child-care, personal freedom and health care. The Dutch press, however, has noted that it scores below-average when it comes to expenditure for higher education and the economic empowerment of women.

Country of Mild Happiness

Nearly 40 years ago, after his long service as a Spanish diplomat in The Hague, the Duke de Baena remarked that the Netherlands is *le pays du petit bonheur* (a country of mild happiness). This is still true today. Most Dutch people are content with and are pleased by their way of life.

Perhaps because of this, however, they also like to dwell on the shortcomings of their society. The ethnic Dutch are quick to complain that even though the Netherlands is already over-populated, more foreigners are being allowed to settle there but are refusing to integrate into Dutch society; the level of common crime is decreasing but that of violent crime is holding steady, chiefly due to high levels of unemployment among ethnic minority youths; traffic congestion is getting worse; and due to a lack of funding, some critically-important national services—education, medical care and train travel— are simply not what they used to be.

There is some truth to all of these assertions but none of these problems appear to be beyond the ability of a prosperous, disciplined and well-organised society to handle. Despite their complaints, the Dutch themselves do like living in the Netherlands; most foreigners will too.

A Gentle People

A Canadian professor working at the Free University of Amsterdam put his finger on one of the basic reasons for this. With a nice turn of phrase, he explained, "There's no undercurrent of violence here. When I go back to the US, people ask me what it's like in the Netherlands. I always tell them it's a gentle society. That's the word that really sums it up for me—gentle."

SOCIAL WELFARE: THE SAFETY NET

Since the end of World War II, the Dutch have created a far-reaching and very generous social welfare system, largely financed by revenues from natural gas. It is one of the most comprehensive in the European Union. While quite complex and vulnerable to abuses, this system includes, among other things, unemployment benefits, housing allowances, child support, paid sick leave, income support, old age benefits and insurance for health care. There is, in short, a virtually unbreakable social welfare safety net designed to catch people before they fall into utter destitution.

Insurance Programmes and Social Services

There are four national insurance programmes and four employee insurance schemes. Buttressing this system are other important social services, for example, the General Family Allowance Act (this helps families support their children up to the age of 18) and the National Assistance Act (which helps those with no or minimal income).

The total cost of all these programmes is now so high that benefits must be administered more tightly if the country is to afford them. One immediate result has been that people who had not been working because of spurious physical or mental ailments have now had to go back to work, either full-time or part-time, if they cannot prove they are genuinely ill.

Nevertheless, as a general rule, any person who has previously worked in the Netherlands but is now involuntarily unemployed will be supported at public expense—although possibly at a low level—while he or she is looking for another job.

A HEALTHY ECONOMY

The Netherlands is among the richest countries of the European Union (EU). In 2006, its gross domestic product (GDP) was the third highest in the EU (after Luxembourg and Ireland). That year, the average income in the Netherlands was 25 per cent higher than the overall EU average.

A highly-industrialised country which also has a strong agricultural sector, the Netherlands is pre-eminently a trading nation and plays a central role in the economic life of Western Europe. (*See* Chapter 9: Doing Business in the Netherlands *on pages 158–170 for more details.*)

At the same time, it is also a 'post-industrial era' power because about 64 per cent of its work force is employed in the service sector. Unemployment is now at 3.2 per cent—a four-year low. Many jobs—both full time and 'flexi-work'—are held by women.

On the industrial front, three of the world's biggest multinational corporations are located here—Royal Dutch Shell, Unilever and Philips. Manufacturing employs about 29 per cent of the labour force (the metal industry is the largest employer here); food, beverage and tobacco manufacturing enterprises rank second in terms of employment but first in production value. The petroleum products, chemical and electrical/electronics industries are also important: BP, Exxon and Texaco, among others, have major refineries or petrochemical plants in the Netherlands.

Intensive agriculture, especially dairy farming and horticulture, is another success story. The highly-mechanised agricultural sector employs just a small percentage of the workforce but produces large surpluses for domestic food

A Dutch dairy farm: agriculture still plays an important role in the economy.

World's Largest Flower Auction

Everyday the world's biggest flower auction (Aalsmeer), which covers an area equal to 75 football fields, ships about 19 million cut flowers and two million potted plants around the globe.

processing and for export. The Netherlands ranks very high in agricultural export value. The milk yield per cow is among the highest in the world; much of it is processed into butter, cheese, or condensed milk and exported. Huge numbers of pigs, calves and chickens are raised in sheds to produce meat and eggs. Hothouse vegetables and flowers are grown under acres of glass, while other vegetables, fruits, flowers, plants and bulbs are produced outdoors in meticulously-cultivated fields.

Given the Netherlands' geographical location, it is natural that for many centuries international trade has been a key component of the economy. Indeed, the value of Dutch imports and exports hovers at around 50–60 per cent of the GDP, a proportion far greater than that of the US or UK. Much of the Netherlands' trade is with Europe and North America. About 75 per cent of Dutch exports go to the EU; most imports come in from Germany, followed by those from the EU and the US.

The Netherlands is thus a gateway for the flow of goods between Western Europe and the rest of the world. These arrive at well-equipped Dutch harbours: Europoort, the port area between Rotterdam and the North Sea, can accommodate the deepest-draft ocean-going ships, while Rotterdam itself handles more tonnage than any other port in the world. Goods continue on their final destination by river boat, train, truck or petroleum pipeline.

MODERATE TRADE UNIONS

As 'social partners' working together with management and government, Dutch trade unions negotiate conditions of work, salary increases and holidays. Although the unions are still influential, their days of greatest power are probably now behind them. They feel they have an important stake in the existing economic order and in recent years, they have held wage demands to moderate levels—on the premise that it is better to let economic growth lead to more jobs

The Royal Family: (L to R, back) Prince Constantijn, Princess Laurentine holding her daughter Leonore, Princess Maxima, Prince Willem-Alexander with his daughter Princess Ariane, Queen Beatrix. (L to R, front) Eloise and her brother Claus-Casimir, Princess Catharina-Amalia and her sister Princess Alexia pose during a photo session in the Austrian skiing resort of Lech in February 2008.

tomorrow rather than more pay today. The outcome is that there are very few strikes in the Netherlands.

Union membership rose more or less steadily from the end of World War II until the worldwide recession precipitated by the oil crisis of 1973. Since then, however, the internationalisation of financial markets and of trade itself have strengthened management's hand and weakened labour's. Only 27 per cent of Dutch workers now belong to unions. In every EU country outside Scandinavia (except Belgium), trade union membership is either static or continues to decline.

THE POLITICS OF ACCOMMODATION

The Netherlands is a parliamentary democracy under a constitutional monarch, Queen Beatrix of the House of Orange-Nassau. In general, this political system works extremely well. Politicians are respected and trusted, more often than not; the queen herself and the rest of the royal family are universally popular.

Since none of the many political parties can get a clear majority, coalition governments, based on the principles of tolerance and consensus, are the rule.

Under the constitution, as revised in 1848, government ministers are accountable to an elected parliament rather than to the monarch. This legislative body, known as the *Staten-Generaal* (States-General), has two houses. The First Chamber (75 members) is elected by the Provincial States. The Second Chamber (150 members) is directly elected; with as little as 0.66 per cent of the total vote, a very small party or political movement can win a seat here.

Both houses share power with the government and control its policies. But since the views of all players in the political arena must be accommodated, a consensus is necessary. In many ways this is a good thing but in practice, much legislation undergoes so many amendments and refinements while it is being drafted that, as a Dutch newspaper complained, "a law designed to achieve a perfectly commendable goal thus quickly becomes an impenetrable tangle of clauses and sub-clauses."

The 443 municipalities (*gemeenten*) are important institutions of local government and are now getting the freedom to manage their own affairs. Presided over by a *burgemeester* (mayor), they are led by a directly elected council made up of 7–45 members. Local standards for law and order are usually set by a 'policy triangle' consisting of a mayor, a public prosecutor and a chief of police.

Flexibility is the hallmark here: the police, for example, are usually instructed to ignore the sale or use of soft drugs and to focus instead on more serious criminal offences. This is a classic example of the traditional Dutch policy of *gedogen*, a word which literally means 'to tolerate'. It is a policy under which certain offences which are punishable by law are not, in practice, prosecuted. Good examples are euthanasia and the use of soft drugs.

MILITARY FORCES: SMALL BUT EFFECTIVE

National defence is provided by the Netherlands' small but well-trained and extremely well-equipped professional military forces, which participate frequently in NATO exercises and play an active role in the UN's international peacekeeping operations.

The police in Amsterdam and other Dutch cities tend to take a comparatively lenient approach to 'soft' drugs so that they can focus their effort on more serious criminal offences.

Conscription in the Netherlands ended in 1996, so all the members of the armed forces are paid professionals. Dutch military forces total about 52,000 men and women. About 8.4 per cent are women, a figure which is expected to rise to 12 per cent by 2020. The armed forces are divided into four key units:

- Royal Navy   11,000 armed forces and 4,000 civilians
- Royal Ground Forces   22,000 armed forces and 8,000 civilians
- Royal Air Force   11,000 armed forces and 1,700 civilians

- Royal Marechaussee   6,000 armed forces and 500 civilians (The Marechaussee is a military police force which controls the country's borders and airports and guards the royal palaces.)

WATER CONTROL BOARDS

One of the oldest and historically most important democratic institutions in the Netherlands is the local Water Control Board. These boards have the crucial task of protecting the land from flooding. They are also responsible for irrigation, drainage and water purification projects and for maintaining the canals and rivers. The senior officers of the boards used to be appointed by the Crown, but are now publicly elected.

FOREIGN POLICY: NEUTRALITY, REALISM AND IDEALISM

As a trading nation, the Netherlands was committed to a strict neutrality and was able to maintain its position during World War I. It tried to pursue the same policy when World War II broke out but the German invasion in 1940 made this impossible. After the war, the security threat posed by the Soviet Union prompted the Netherlands to put neutrality aside and to join NATO. It is now a member of many other international organisations, including the UN, the EU, the Organisation of Economic Cooperation and Development (OECD), the Western European Union, and the Council of Europe.

Because the Dutch have a very strong commitment to helping those less fortunate than themselves, 'development cooperation' (i.e. foreign aid) is an integral part of Dutch foreign policy. The Netherlands provides assistance and expertise to many developing countries and was the second country (after Sweden) to achieve the internationally agreed aim of giving at least 0.7 per cent of its Gross National Product (GNP) in this process.

DRUGS: SOFT AND HARD

A 'coffee shop' is a café where soft drugs are sold, subject to certain restrictions: no hard drugs may be sold; drugs may not be advertised; the 'coffee shop' must not disturb the peace; no drugs may be sold to persons under 18 and no minors are allowed on the premises. The Dutch tolerate limited sales of soft drugs for personal consumption because, they explain, this lets the police concentrate on suppressing trafficking and consumption of hard drugs, such as heroin and cocaine, and keeps soft drug users outside the criminal circuit.

But in response to domestic and international criticisms of these permissive drug policies (the French have denounced the Netherlands as 'a drug state' and as 'a paradise for drug tourists'), the Dutch government decided in 1996 to reduce from 30 to 5 g per customer the amount of soft drugs which can legally be sold in the 'coffee shops' of Amsterdam and other cities. The number of coffee shops in Amsterdam, which had increased so rapidly in the 1980s (from nine in 1980 to 101 in 1988), has now declined as well.

Hard Drugs

It bears repeating here that in the big Dutch cities there is a good deal of petty, opportunistic theft. Much of this is related to the use of hard drugs: addicts (the Dutch refer to them as *junks*) steal things which they can sell quickly in order to buy the drugs they need to stave off the agonies of withdrawal.

In Europe, the Netherlands is an important transfer and distribution country for heroin, cocaine and cannabis and also produces synthetic drugs. The use of hard and soft drugs by the Dutch has remained stable over the past ten years. About 5.5 per cent of the population uses cannabis; hard drugs (ecstasy, cocaine and heroin) are used by only 1.5 per cent.

The Dutch say that tighter control of drug runners at Schiphol Airport has been a success. Over the last few years, hundreds of suspected drug runners have been arrested and hundreds of kilograms of cocaine have been confiscated. The number of drug runners per flight has decreased due to the introduction of strict controls for 'high-risk flights' i.e. flights favoured by drug runners.

Despite all the criticisms they have received, the Dutch remain convinced their policy of paying less attention to soft drugs and more to suppressing hard drugs is paying off handsomely. The proof of the pudding, they might say, is that according to a Dutch institute that monitors heroin addicts, addicts are 'a dying breed'.

KEEP TRACK OF YOUR WORLDLY GOODS

Shoplifting and pocket-picking are the most common urban crimes. But new or expensive bicycles are also certain to disappear unless carefully secured with heavy-duty locks. Even well-locked bikes run the risk of having their wheels kicked in if they are left unattended in certain areas. Householders also take pains to make sure they have secure locks on all their doors. In Amsterdam, parked cars are broken into so frequently and their radios stolen so often that some cars display notices informing potential thieves that 'There is no radio in this car'.

It is important to remember that violent crimes are not common. Though they have increased over the last ten years, they account for only a small percentage of the total crimes. This means that the Netherlands remains one of the least violent countries in the world.

The bottom line is that you will probably not be murdered or mugged in the Netherlands and that if you keep a close watch on your bicycle, car radio (just be careful where you park) and other worldly goods, they are not likely to disappear.

DUTCH CUSTOMS

You will understand the Dutch more easily if you know a little bit about some of their customs and habits. These would certainly include preserving the past; a reliance on rules and regulations; cleanliness; traditional food and drink; smoking; sorting rubbish; the importance of birthdays.

Known the world over, these wooden clogs have become a symbol of the Netherlands to people from other parts of the world. Ironically, the Dutch do not have strong feelings about them.

Artifacts of a Treasured Past

The Dutch of today do not worship the past but they certainly respect it and want to keep many parts of it alive.

They may not have any strong feelings about clogs (the traditional wooden shoes), although these are in fact quite useful for gardening because they do keep your feet warm and dry. Nor do they wax ecstatic about the colourful traditional Dutch costumes, such as those still worn by men, women and children in a handful of Dutch villages.

Such artifacts may provide great photo opportunities for the tourists who come to the Netherlands from all over

Café Hoppe in Amsterdam (built in 1670) is without doubt the most authentic brown café in the city centre. For as long as anyone can remember, the interior of this standing room only bar has remained virtually unchanged. This is probably the reason for its popularity. Hoppe sells more beer per sq m than any other café in the Netherlands.

the world but the Dutch themselves do not think of them as being vitally important aspects of their national culture. What the Dutch do think worth cherishing and preserving at all costs are:

- The important natural features of their country, such as the De Hoge Veluwe National Park and the Wadden Islands, which can best be preserved by sensitive environmental management techniques.
- The extensive architectural heritage of the Netherlands. Into this category the Dutch would put all the fine old houses, historic streets, cafés, ships, dykes, canals, windmills, churches and traditional farmhouses.

RULES AND REGULATIONS

A labyrinth of complicated rules and regulations protects almost all of this architectural heritage. Official planning permission is needed to make any significant changes to it and approval is not given lightly or quickly. Indeed, property owners can sometimes find themselves caught between conflicting official demands.

Take the *bruine cafes* ('brown cafés'), for example. These are old Dutch drinking spots darkened by decades or even centuries of tobacco smoke. One of the most famous in Amsterdam is Café Hoppe in a city square known as *het Spui* ('the sluice'). This café opened its doors for business in 1670 and the Dutch have been drinking and smoking there ever since.

Door Dilemma

But there are a good number of less ancient brown cafés, too. The owner of one of them recounted the problems he was having with the front door of his café.

This brown café stands on a corner where two Amsterdam streets meet—let us call them Street A and B. For many years their front door had opened onto Street A. At one point, however, the owner was told that to comply with new fire regulations, his front door had to be moved so that it opened onto Street B. Planning permission officials, however, insisted that the front door had to remain facing Street A—but that to restore the café's historic authenticity, the door would have to be relocated so that it was closer to the corner!

CLEANLINESS AND GODLINESS

If the Dutch homes are not the very cleanest in the world, they must certainly be very close to being the cleanest. It may be stretching the point a bit to say that the Dutch have always tacitly considered cleanliness to be more important than godliness, but traditionally these two qualities have gone hand-in-hand.

A clean house, for example—so clean that the window curtains were always left open to show off the interior—was indisputable proof that a respectable Calvinist family lived within. Stripped of its religious overtones, this social pressure continues today. Curtains are still left open and most middle-class housewives believe that maintenance standards in the home must be kept very high; if they are not, the neighbours would surely talk.

A TOBACCO CULTURE

The paintings of the Golden Age show us that a Dutchman of that era, taking his ease in a tavern or at home, was rarely without his long-stemmed clay pipe. In more recent times the Dutch have continued to be avid smokers. If you are a nonsmoker, you may find it ironic that despite the fact that the Dutch are very health-conscious on the whole, their houses, flats, restaurants and bars are rarely smoke-free. In 2008, all restaurants and pubs will be smoke-free.

PROTECT THE ENVIRONMENT: SORT YOUR RUBBISH

Environmental protection is a vitally important issue in the Netherlands because the country is so small and so densely populated. As a result, the Dutch have become a very disciplined people when it comes to sorting their rubbish.

They are required by law (and you will be too) to separate rubbish into specific categories—organic materials, inorganic substances, glass, paper, and chemical wastes (paint, batteries, etc)—and to put it into separate bins. Deposit glass (used in soft drink and beer bottles and for which you are charged money) is returned to specified sites for cash or credit. About 75 per cent of the non-deposit glass is recycled for other uses.

NEVER FORGET A BIRTHDAY

For the Dutch (young and old alike), birthdays are major cultural events. Forgetting a birthday is such a major blunder that in most Dutch homes, you will find a 'birthday calendar' hanging on the door of the toilet, where it can be pondered on frequently and at leisure.

To celebrate his or her birthday, a child may get presents in the morning. He or she will bring candy to school to give to other children. Later in the day, parents always give a party for the child. The whole family comes and joins in happy birthday songs and ritualised congratulations to the fortunate child.

In a marked departure from the custom in some other countries, an adult celebrates his or her own birthday by inviting other people over for drinks or by giving a birthday party. And if you are working in an office, you are even expected to bring birthday cakes to the office so that your colleagues can participate in this festive occasion too.

HOW SHOULD FOREIGNERS BEHAVE IN THE NETHERLANDS?

You should keep in mind that Dutch society revolves around three simple themes:

- Tolerance
  Letting people do things their own way as long as they do not disturb others.
- Honesty and straightforwardness
  When you say 'yes' or 'no', you must mean precisely that, not 'maybe', 'perhaps' or 'we shall see later on'. This is important because in many other cultures it is considered extremely impolite to give a blunt 'yes' or 'no' answer. If you happen to come from one of these cultures, you must now begin to practise the painfully direct Dutch approach.
- Hospitality
  Making a guest feel comfortable and at home.

Major Social Sins

You can immediately understand from this short list that a foreigner who wants to get along well with the Dutch must make every effort not to come across as prejudiced, devious or antisocial. These are major sins which are not easily forgiven.

Lesser Social Sins

Although the Dutch usually like foreigners on a one-to-one basis, they do not appreciate group tourism because it is noisy and brings out what they consider to be some of the foreigners' less desirable traits. These the Dutch would list as flashiness, over-confidence, self-assertiveness, boisterous behaviour and bragging about wealth. You would do very well to avoid these failings too.

In this connection and taking a page out of classical history, a Dutch journalist in Amsterdam once joked that some of his colleagues considered the Americans, in all their pride and economic, cultural and military might, to be 'the new Romans' of our era. In contrast, he continued, the Dutch like to think of themselves as 'the old Greeks'—that is, as a much better-educated and more highly cultured people who are no longer at the centre of world affairs.

Greeting Each Other

People shake hands very frequently in the Netherlands and a short, warm, firm handshake is more valued than a long, tepid limp-wristed grip. When you come into a room, shake hands with all the adults you know. You will probably quickly be introduced to the others but if not, you can introduce yourself by name and with a handshake.

Good friends usually greet each other by kissing each other, very lightly, on the cheeks two or three times, first on one side and then on the other. (This is actually not so much a real kiss as it is a quick touching of cheeks.) In any case, there is one important exception to this: although men may kiss women and women may kiss each other, heterosexual men never kiss other men.

LIVING IN THE NETHERLANDS

'If you look at the manners of everyday life, there is no race more open to humanity and kindness or less given to wildness or ferocious behavior. It is a straightforward nature, without treachery or deceit and not prone to any serious vices except, that is, a little given to pleasure, especially to feasting. The reason for this is, I think, the wonderful supply of everything that can tempt one to enjoyment; due partly to the ease of importing goods and partly to the natural fertility of the region...'
—Renaissance humanist Desiderius Erasmus

THIS CHAPTER IS A POTPOURRI of practical information which will hopefully be useful to you from the moment you first decide to move to the Netherlands. It covers a wide range of areas:

- Getting a good start
- Housing
- Travel: by air, land and water
- Documents needed
- Money matters
- Medical care
- Telecommunications and electrical equipment
- Leisure activities
- Religion
- Pets

GETTING A GOOD START

The ideal way to find your footing quickly in the Netherlands is to have Dutch friends who are willing to help and advise you. But it can take some time to make friends so it is never too early to start looking for them.

One very good reason to start early is that if you are like most people, your second or third month in any foreign country may well prove to be the most difficult. By then the initial starry-eyed excitement of travel to and arrival in the Netherlands will have worn off but you will not yet have had time to find your own particular niche in Dutch society. So making a concerted effort in the first month to make some Dutch friends may pay big dividends later on.

Fortunately, it is quite easy to meet people in the Netherlands. The Dutch like to live very busy lives but neighbours, office colleagues or local officials can always find time to answer your questions or point you in the right direction. Virtually all of them will speak at least some English and, being world travellers, most of them are also quite interested in foreigners. Indeed, it is likely that many of the people you meet will already have visited your own country.

One can recommend a three-step approach to integrating yourself into Dutch society:

- meet your neighbours
- get in touch with some of the many social organisations designed to help newcomers to the Netherlands
- join a Dutch sports club

This three-pronged approach cannot, of course, guarantee that you will make some good Dutch friends but the chances of this happening are rather high. What is certain is that if you merely sit around waiting for the Dutch to come to you, your tour of duty in the Netherlands may be over before they do.

Step One: Meet Your Neighbours

A French lady once moved to another West European country (not the Netherlands). After several years there, she still had not met her next-door neighbour. So one fine morning, she decided to knock on the neighbour's door and introduce herself. Being fluent in the local language, she was able to do this with the utmost politeness, "Good morning, madame," she said, "I am your next-door neighbour." Imagine her surprise when her neighbour said to her brusquely, "Well, what is it that you want?"

Such a reply would be unheard of in the Netherlands. Indeed, it is up to you to make the first move. Your Dutch neighbours will not force themselves upon you but they will naturally be curious about you and will be very pleased if you take the first opportunity to introduce yourself and tell them where you are from and why you are in their country.

It is certainly appropriate for you to invite them to your own house for coffee (at almost any time of the day, but around 10:30 am is best) or for a drink in the evening. But to avoid any cross-cultural misunderstanding, you should not use a 'California-style' invitation—that is, a vague invitation cast in such general terms ("Do come see us!") that it is really only an expression of goodwill rather than a firm social commitment. Instead, try to find a mutually convenient date and time while you are first talking with your new neighbour.

Step Two: Get in Touch with a Social Organisation for Foreigners

Your own embassy, consulate or company may well have some good suggestions on living in the Netherlands but the international women's clubs are likely to be even better sources of information. They also offer a wide variety of social activities where you can easily 'meet-and-greet' other people, foreigners and Dutch alike.

Fortunately, there is no shortage of these clubs. To list just a few of them: the American Women's Club, the British Women's Club, the Petroleum Wives Club, the Australian and New Zealand Women's Club and the international women's association known as Contact.

ACCESS

One social organisation in The Hague which has been highly recommended is ACCESS (the Administrative Committee to Coordinate English-Speaking Services). Located at Societeit de Witte, Plein 24, 2511 CS The Hague, ACCESS is a non-profit organisation staffed by English-speaking multinational volunteers. In addition to social functions, among the many support activities it offers are advice on settling in, counselling services and information on language development for bilingual children.

Step Three: Join a Dutch Sports Club

Even if you are not keen on participating in sports yourself, one of the very best ways to meet the Dutch is to join one of their sports clubs. Some other countries may have an extensive network of sports facilities which are open to the public but this is usually not the case in the Netherlands. As a general rule, to participate in a sport here, you must be a member or a guest of a local sports club. This is why, in such a small country, there are about 30,000 sports clubs with a total membership of more than four million people.

In descending order of size, the major clubs are those devoted to fishing, football (i.e. soccer, the Dutch national sport), tennis, and field hockey. But there are also clubs for almost all other activities, for example, water sports (sail and power boating, canoeing, surfing, swimming, boat trips and water skiing), cycling, horseback riding, hiking, steam trains, ice skating, bird watching, caravan trips, golf and automobile and motorcycle racing. For the more sedentary, card clubs are very popular too.

HOUSING

The Netherlands is the most densely populated country in Europe. It already has a large number of single households and this number is increasing rapidly because more people are choosing not to marry, while others are deciding to divorce.

The availability of housing is a huge problem, especially in big cities such as Amsterdam, The Hague, Rotterdam and Utrecht. It is also a problem in smaller cities where many university students live; Leiden and Groningen are good examples. Housing is therefore very difficult (but not impossible) to find. Rental prices will, of course, vary considerably but in good locations, they will be at least equal to—and probably more than—what you would have to pay in a comparable British or American city.

Rental accommodation is often advertised in local newspapers. One can also rent through an estate agent or via the website www.funda.nl. Noticeboards in shops and supermarkets, and word of mouth, are also important sources of information. The Wednesday edition of the daily newspaper *De Telegraaf* has many advertisements for accommodation. Rental properties are normally unfurnished and the rent is paid monthly. Landlords will normally require a deposit of one month's rent. Contracts are usually valid for indefinite periods, unless otherwise agreed. At least

Elegant mansions were initially built as private residences but are now often used as offices or museums.

one month's notice is required before you leave. Generally speaking, there is very good rent protection for tenants. The value of houses is officially calculated on a system of points. If a landlord exceeds the yearly rent increase or otherwise fails to carry out his responsibilities, a renter can have recourse to an independent rent tribunal (*Huurcommissie*), which is regulated by the government.

Left to their own devices, most of the Dutch—especially those with young children—would much prefer to live in a small, well-built semi-detached house with a garden in one of the many charming towns on the fringes of the big cities. In practice, however, for financial or other reasons (commuting, for example) many people decide instead to live in flats (apartments) located within or close to the city where they work. These flats can be found in both modern purpose-built structures and in big older homes which have been carved up into smaller units.

Renting vs Buying

Because of the high transaction cost involved (taxes, etc) it may not make financial sense to buy a place of your own unless you plan to live in the Netherlands for more than, say, three years. Renting is a perfectly acceptable alternative.

Traditional Dutch houses are carefully maintained.

Indeed, until recently more than half the Dutch lived in rented accommodations. Today, however, they are more inclined to buy rather than rent a house. One reason is that the Netherlands, compared with other EU countries, still has the most generous tax breaks on mortgages.

Location, Location, Location

As in any country, these are the three rules of finding a good place to live. It is up to you to do your homework (friends and colleagues can help you here) and get at least a rough idea just where you would like to live so you can identify the area by name; for example, "I would like to see some houses in Wassenaar." (This is a posh town close to The Hague which is favoured by senior executives.)

Your Estate Agent

To rent or buy housing, you will almost certainly need the services of a *makelaar* (estate agent). Your neighbours, friends or office colleagues are likely to know someone in this business, which is probably the best way to find a competent estate agent. But you can also come in off the street and talk with an estate agent whose office is located near where you would like to live.

Because your stay in the Netherlands might be curtailed by forces beyond your control—job transfers, illnesses, family problems, etc—it is important to make sure there is a 'diplomatic clause' in any rental agreement you sign. This will let you move out of the house on two months' notice.

Dutch Houses

So many things are small-scaled in the Netherlands that you should not be surprised to find that, except for the few merchant mansions or stately homes still in private hands, most Dutch houses are relatively small. If you are used to living in a big house filled with big furniture, you may feel a bit cramped at first but this feeling will soon pass.

There may be one exception, however—the very steep staircases which are so common in older Dutch homes will not get any easier to negotiate. These traditional stairs, in

fact, are the reason Dutch craftsmen made sure that the heavy, ornately-carved wooden cabinets they built could be disassembled easily. Once a cabinet was in pieces it could be hoisted from the street to a window on an upper floor by means of a pulley attached to a beam projecting from the top of the house.

Dutch houses are usually offered for rent unfurnished and to an American or British eye, they may seem spartan in the extreme. For example, they may need wallpapering or interior repainting. They will not have any household appliances, floor coverings, curtains, lamps, etc. There may not be any built-in lighting fixtures.

If you want a few more worldly goods in your new home, look for semi-furnished housing instead, which may well have light fixtures, some kitchen appliances and fitted carpets.

You can, of course, move into a fully furnished home without having to provide too many things yourself besides bed linen and towels.

Because stairways in old Dutch houses are very steep and narrow, beams projecting from the roofs were used to lift furniture and other heavy objects.

DOMESTIC HELP

Because the Netherlands is such a prosperous and highly egalitarian society, almost no one has live-in servants. For most people, a nanny is prohibitively expensive because an employer must pay not only her salary but also her social security coverage. Traditionally, Dutch mothers stayed at home to care for their children. These days, however, most have flexi-jobs and work between 16–24 hours a week. Childcare facilities are expensive, but only one-third of the cost has to be paid by the parents. The remainder is paid by the mother's employer and/or by the government. There is a shortage of childcare facilities because not too many people are interested in this line of work. You can, however, find part-time cleaning ladies through advertisements in the local newspapers.

TRAVEL: BY AIR, LAND AND WATER

Perhaps because the Dutch are Europe's greatest travellers, they have taken pains to make sure that travel to, from and within the Netherlands itself is safe, fast, efficient, well-organised and affordable. Their public transportation is, in a word, excellent: it is certainly one of the best systems in the world.

Travel by Air

The biggest Dutch airport is Schiphol, located south-west of Amsterdam and built on the bed of a former lake (the Haarlemmermeer) which was drained at the turn of the century and transformed into a polder, that is, into prime agricultural land.

Founded in 1919, KLM is the oldest international airline in the world. The Amsterdam-London line, first flown by KLM in 1920, is the oldest air route still served by the same airline. KLM recently merged with Air France. The KLM group and its partners now serve a global network connecting more than 217 destinations in 85 countries on six continents. It is an outstandingly efficient, clean, user-friendly airport with good shops and good food. It offers easy access to Dutch and other European cities via a dense network of motorways and railways. There is even a railway station within the terminal itself.

The Schiphol Airport in Amsterdam.

Schiphol has become so popular, especially with transit passengers who account for nearly 40 per cent of total passenger movements, that the Dutch have drawn up ambitious but environmentally-sensitive plans to expand it into a Mainport, i.e. a hub of intercontinental and European air, road and rail traffic.

It is hoped that once high-speed trains (see the next section on 'Trains') are in wider use in the Netherlands, travellers bound for other European cities will decide to go by rail rather than by air, thus reducing the passenger burden on Schiphol itself.

International airlines offer regular services to some other airports in the Netherlands as well—to Rotterdam, Eindhoven and Maastricht. More and more companies are using Lelystad Airport (about 30 miles north-east of Amsterdam) for business flights to destinations within Europe. This new airport, which will grow into a regional airport over the next few years, will also offer scheduled flights, flying lessons, sightseeing flights and aircraft rentals.

Travel by Land
Trains

Although service has deteriorated somewhat as a result of privatisation and under-investment, the Netherlands still has a good railway network. With nearly 400 stations, it is the most closely-knit in Europe and can boast of clean, fast, modern trains (many with snacks and refreshments on offer) linking all parts of the country. At least two trains an hour operate on each route; four to six trains per hour run between the major cities. Indeed, nearly every place in the Netherlands is accessible by train.

Since English is so widely spoken it is quite easy to travel by train. One of the best innovations is a useful service one can describe as 'computerised directions'. This is how it works:

Let us assume that you live in Amsterdam but have an appointment in Rotterdam at a given time. When you buy a ticket, if you tell the ticket agent when you have to be in Rotterdam, he or she will upon request give you not only a ticket but also a free computer printout showing the arrival and departure times of the most convenient trains for your journey, their track numbers and the details of any interstation transfers you may have to make.

Armed with this handy printout, you can turn your attention to other more interesting matters, rather than worrying about the logistics of rail travel.

Regular tickets can be bought at the *Binnenland* (domestic) ticket office at every Dutch station or from ticket machines. There are first- and second-class seats; a day-return trip ticket is always cheaper than two single tickets.

Rail passes and special discounts are widely available. The *Euro Domino* pass, available from the *Internationaal* (international) ticket office at any one of 60 main stations, gives you three, five or ten days of unlimited rail travel in the Netherlands. Day tickets give you a day's unlimited travel, while *Rail Idee* (rail idea) tickets are available for visits to

Second-class railway carriage: clean, comfortable and fast.

Central railway station in Amsterdam.

museums and other tourist attractions. Senior citizens and children get special fares too.

Another excellent innovation is the *Treintaxi* (train-taxi), available at more than 38 railway stations serving several hundred villages, towns and cities (except for Amsterdam, Rotterdam and The Hague, where you can take local taxis).

Treintaxi tickets can be bought only at railway ticket offices, not in the taxi itself. When you buy your ticket you pay a small additional fixed charge. A taxi will be at your destination and will deliver you to any address in the surrounding area. Since you will be sharing the taxi with other travellers going to different addresses, the cost per person is quite low. Treintaxi tickets now sell for 4.30 euros if you already have a train ticket and 5 euros if you do not. To reserve a taxi, call 0900-8734682.

The Dutch are improving their railway network all the time. In 2007, a new high speed rail connection, known as the HSL (Hoge Snelheids Lijn), will link the Randstad with Belgium and France. It will take only one hour and 45 minutes to get from Amsterdam to Brussels and only two and a half hours to go from Rotterdam to Paris.

Automobiles

If you live in the heart of Amsterdam or in one of the other big cities, you can get by without owning a car because the public transportation network is so good. Not having a car will spare you the experience of Dutch traffic jams, which are bad now and are expected to get even worse as the number of cars on the road increases.

Outside the big cities, however, a car is really quite useful. A wide range of makes and models is available but prices are high and repairs, insurance, road tax and petrol are all expensive. As a result, the smaller European or Japanese cars are more popular than big American vehicles. If you decide to rent a car, remember that almost all rental cars are equipped with manual rather than automatic transmissions.

If you want to bring your present car with you, first check to confirm that it can be brought in duty-free as part of your household goods. Also make sure that it is a type already in use in the Netherlands. Otherwise, you may find it expensive and very time-consuming (up to one year) to get it registered.

Driving Licence and Insurance

If you are a national of an EU country, you may use your valid national driving licence for up to ten years after you arrive in the Netherlands. If you are not from the EU, an international driving licence might be required and you will have to exchange your driving licence for a Dutch licence within 185 days after arrival. If you are more than 70 years old, you will need a medical test. Always check with Town Hall (Gemeentehuis) in the place where you will reside, or check the RDW (Rijksdienst voor Wegverkeer) site http://www.rdw.nl. Click on 'international visitor'. If you bring a car into the Netherlands or buy one there, you will need third party insurance (this is required by law) but more comprehensive insurance cover is strongly recommended. The minimum age for driving is 18 for cars and 16 for mopeds.

The ANWB

You should consider becoming a member of a truly excellent organisation for motorists (and for tourists, cyclists and caravaners as well)—the Royal Dutch Touring Association, known as the ANWB. Its affiliate, the Wegenwacht (WW) patrols the main roads and will assist you if your car breaks down. It will respond to telephone calls from the emergency roadside telephones. The ANWB also provides technical inspections, legal advice and very good maps.

Once equipped with a car, licence and insurance, you are ready to sally forth onto Dutch roads. Fortunately, driving in the Netherlands poses no special risks or challenges for the newcomer who is used to driving in other developed countries.

Traffic moves on the right. Traffic emerging from the right (including bicycles and mopeds) has the right of way. Most Dutch drivers are competent and disciplined, perhaps more so in the country than in the frustratingly heavy traffic of the cities. One of the drivers' few bad habits is impatience: they do not make allowances for drivers who may not know precisely how to get where they are going. Tailgating (following behind a car too closely) can be another fault.

Speed Limits

There are 2,360 km (1,466 miles) of toll-free motorways (*autosnelweg*). Many of these roads are surprisingly quiet because a special macadam mixture is used to reduce tyre noise. The maximum speed limit is either 120 kmph (74 mph) or 100 kmph (62 mph), depending on the area. Other speed limits are 50 kmph (31 mph) in built-up areas and 80 kmph (49 mph) on provincial roads.

Speed limits are enforced by police on fast BMW motorcycles, backed up by numerous speed traps and radar detectors. Fines are high if you are caught speeding and you can lose your licence as well. During weekends and holidays, there are many checks for alcohol, drugs and weapons.

Caravans

Caravans (house trailers) are exceptionally popular in the Netherlands because they provide convenient low-cost family accommodation on long trips and for vacations. The Dutch are the greatest users of caravans in Europe and are possibly the most expert and the most friendly. It is easy for foreigners to join them: you can either rent a caravan in the Netherlands or bring your own. The documentation valid in the caravan's country of origin is all that is required.

Well-organised in this as in all their other leisure pursuits, Dutch caravaners will almost certainly be members of one of the many caravan clubs in their country. If they want to buy a second-hand caravan, the ANWB stands ready to give them technical advice on its particular strengths and weaknesses.

Bus, Tram and Metro

For those coming to the Netherlands from countries where public transportation is either spotty or non-existent, using the well-ordered Dutch 'zone' network of buses and trams and the metro (the latter in Amsterdam or Rotterdam only) will be an eye-opening experience.

The cheapest way to ride on a bus or tram or on the metro is to buy a *strippenkaart* (strips ticket) from post offices, newsagents, tobacconists, train stations, supermarkets or from the offices of the Netherlands' tourist information centre, abbreviated as VVV (Vereniging voor Vreemdelingenverkeer), one of which is conveniently located opposite Amsterdam's central railway station. This ticket consists of a number of individual *strippen* (strips); the more strips you buy at one time, the cheaper your travel is.

The entire *strippenkaart* system is so complicated that the best thing to do is to ask a Dutch friend or colleague to explain it. For short trips you can pay the bus or tram driver directly, even though this is more expensive than using a *strippenkaart*. The good news is that in 2009, the new *OV-chipkaart*, a credit card-sized replacement for all public transport tickets and *strippenkaarten*, will come into use. There will be an *OV-chipkaart* for tourists too.

Bicycles

The Netherlands now has about 18 million bikes—more than one per person in the country. Cycling is such an important part of Dutch life that it is worth discussing it in some detail.

If you already have a bike, by all means bring it with you. If you do not, even if you do not normally ride a bicycle you should consider buying one (or, for day use, renting one) as soon as possible after your arrival.

The reason is that because the Netherlands is so flat, so small, so congested and has such good bike lanes, a bicycle is a very practical aid to daily life. They are widely used by men and women (young and old alike) and by teenagers and children. Typical uses are commuting to work or school, shopping (most bikes have two big panniers for groceries and many have seats for small children as well) and day or overnight recreational trips.

The Dutch have built a unique and very dense network of over 20,000 km (12,400 miles) of separate bicycle lanes. These

Bicycles are a convenient and environmentally-friendly mode of transport in the Netherlands.

keep bicycles and cars apart, making cycling much safer and certainly much less stressful than it is in other countries.

This network is clearly marked with the ANWB's red and white signs and mushroom-shaped posts, which give the quickest bicycle route from one point to another. Bike paths are also marked by special safety signs, which must be obeyed. For example, a white bicycle on a round blue sign means that both regular bicycles (*fietsen*) and mopeds (*bromfietsen*) may use that lane. On the other hand, a rectangular sign marked *Fietspad* ('bicycle path') indicates that only bicycles (not mopeds) are allowed there.

The sign *Fietsers oversteken* ('bicycles cross here') means that the bike path is about to cross a road used by cars and that both cyclists and motorists must be especially careful. Drivers must at all times watch with the utmost care for children or teenage cyclists. Even though these young people may make sudden unpredictable manoeuvres, they will probably still have the legal right of way.

Dutch bikes and bike shops are of excellent quality. Helmets are not required but all bicycles should have safe handlebars, front and rear lights that work, a functioning bell and a rear mudguard. Most Dutch bicycles come equipped with a built-in lock which secures the rear wheel, but given the very high rate of bike thefts, a heavy chain with a separate lock is a prudent investment. Bike insurance is a good idea too, especially for a new machine.

Bicycles can also be hired for day use in many places in the Netherlands, e.g. at 80 railway stations. Most of these will be workhorse machines with only one gear. This will be sufficient for city use but if you are riding any distance, peddling into the wind or carrying anything heavier than a rain suit, you will find that three gears are very welcome. So if you do buy a bike of your own, make sure it has at least three gears.

Travel by Water
Travel by water is one of the best ways to get to the Netherlands and to enjoy it once you are there. The major ferry ports are Vlissingen, Rotterdam and Hook of Holland

A fine mahogany pleasure launch—a joy to behold and a great way to see the country.

Taking a trip on one of these canal boats is one of the most popular attractions in Amsterdam.

(Hoek van Holland), with many crossings from and to the UK. You can also travel underwater to and from the UK—by train, with or without your car—via the Channel Tunnel.

The English word 'yacht' comes from the Dutch *jacht* and it should come as no surprise that the Dutch love being out on the water. Sailing craft and motor yachts of various shapes and sizes are readily available for sale or rent in the Netherlands.

Many boats for rent have an official one-to-five star classification indicating the facilities they offer. Historic Dutch ships with a great deal of character, most of them flat-bottomed boats skippered by a professional captain, can also be hired. These include the colourful *tjalken* (spritsail barges), *botters* (fishing smacks), schooners and clippers. Motorised, luxuriously converted cargo vessels known as Dutch barges—usually big, narrow, heavy steel boats from 30–50 m (98.4–164 ft) long with the pilot house set far astern—can also be engaged for group charters.

You can take boat trips on Dutch canals, lakes (IJsselmeer) and rivers (Rhine, Maas, Waal and Eastern Scheldt). Excellent boat tours of the port of Rotterdam are offered by the SPIDO company. Its day-long *Deltawerken en zeven rivieren* (Delta Works and seven rivers) trip is also recommended.

DOCUMENTS NEEDED

As a foreigner, obtaining all the necessary paperwork and keeping it in good order is important in any country. The Netherlands is certainly no exception. Indeed, the Dutch are very fond of rules, regulations and red tape—as you will soon find out.

Visa

As a general rule, citizens from EU countries, the US or from certain other countries who are coming to the Netherlands as tourists do not need visas for a stay of up to three months. A valid passport or a valid identity card (for EU citizens) will suffice.

Check with the Embassy or Consulate

Because visa rules and regulations may change, it is essential that you check with the nearest Netherlands embassy or consulate to find out if you do need a visa or a temporary resident permit and if so how to apply for one.

Temporary Residence Permit

For stays of more than three months, a temporary residence permit (*machtiging tot voorlopig verblijf or* MVV) is needed. Exceptions are made for EU nationals and those from some other countries. Many people between 16 and 65 who need an authorization for temporary residence (MVV) in order to live in the Netherlands will first have to take a civic integration examination in their own country of residence. This requirement applies to (among others) people who wish to form a family in the Netherlands (for example, through marriage or by forming a relationship) and to religious leaders coming to the Netherlands for employment as imams or preachers. In many cases, passing this examination becomes an additional condition which must be met before a MVV can be issued.

The examination will test fundamental knowledge of the Dutch language and Dutch society. It is held orally, in Dutch, at the Netherlands embassy or consulate general in the foreign national's country of residence. Taking the examination will cost about 350 euros. The website www. naarnederland.nl is designed to help applicants prepare themselves for this examination. Additional information can be found on the website: http://www.ind.nl.

Place of Application

Please note that if a MVV is needed, it must be applied for at the Netherlands embassy or consulate in your own country or in your country of residence.

Population Register

You may have to go to the Population Register (*Bevolkingsregister*) at the local Town Hall (*Stadhuis*) before you go to the Aliens Police. Call first and find out.

Unless you are a national of one of the countries exempt from these procedures—check with a Netherlands embassy or consulate to find out—a vast amount of paperwork may be required by the Population Register.

This can include not only your own passport but also the rental/purchase agreement on a flat or house in the Netherlands, proof of registration if staying at a hotel, birth certificate, marriage certificate or divorce certificate.

It is essential to note that some of these documents may first have to be authenticated by an Apostille Certificate, which can usually be provided only by the municipality where the document itself was issued. If you were married in your living room in Kathmandu, Nepal—as one of the authors of this book was—getting an Apostille Certificate can pose enormous bureaucratic challenges.

Social Fiscal Number

After you have successfully navigated your way through the reefs and shoals of the Aliens Police and Population Register procedures, you must then apply for a Social Fiscal number (SoFi) if you will be employed in the Netherlands. This number identifies you in the tax and social security system and will be required by any prospective employer or temporary employment agency. Local Dutch tax authorities can advise you on how to do this.

DigiD-code

A DigiD-code is a log-in code that anyone with a Social Fiscal number (SOFI-nummer) can apply for. This log-in code is personalised for the full spectrum of contacts, via the Internet, with such governmental bodies as the Social Insurance Institute (SVB, Sociale Verzekeringsbank), the Centre for Work and Income (CWI, Centrum voor Werk en Inkomen), the Employees' Insurance and Benefits Office (UWV, Uitvoeringsinstituut Werknemersverzekeringen) and the Tax Authorities (Belastingdienst). This authentication allows the authorities to confirm that no one else is acting under your name. With DigiD, the government wants to improve and simplify government Internet services.

Work Permit

Unless you are an EU national, you will need a permit (*werkvergunning*) if you are going to be employed by a company in the Netherlands. Unfortunately, this is not always easy to get. (*For details, see* Chapter 9: Doing Business in the Netherlands *on pages 164–165.*)

MONEY MATTERS

The euro (€) replaced the Netherlands guilder (NLG) as the Dutch national currency on 28 January 2002 (the exchange rate is about NLG 2.20 to 1 euro).

Current euro banknotes are: 500, 200, 100, 50, 20, 10 and 5; and coins: 2 euros, 1 euro, 50, 20, 10, 5, 2 and 1 cent.

As their personal cheques, the Dutch use Eurocheques backed up by a Europas (a cheque guarantee card). When your Dutch bank gives you a Europas, it will also give you a PIN (Personal Identity Number) code. This is extremely useful to have because with it you can get euros 24 hours a day from any automatic cash dispenser (*geldautomaat*). The Dutch also use cash as well as debit and credit cards extensively.

Opening a Bank Account

The regulations for opening a bank account in the Netherlands are rather stringent. It is advisable to visit the bank personally; or better yet, make an appointment so that a bank officer can help with the process. The documents required are:

- valid passport or ID
- MVV, residence permits or other proof of residency (e.g. lease agreement)
- SoFi number
- employment documents or proof of income

Also, for non-EU citizens, you will need your work permit. The banks are likely to check your credit history and then register you with the Central Credit Registration Office (BKR) so that any credit line you apply for will later be registered with them.

The Dutch can pay their bills with bank/Giro forms. A company to whom you owe money may well send you an 'accept giro' form which will already have printed on it your name and the amount to be paid. All you have to do is fill in your bank account number, sign this form and send it to the bank. Or you can make use of telebanking, which has become widely used.

You can also use the Dutch Post Office to pay your bills. The Postbank (will merge with the ING bank in 2009) does most of what a bank does but does not charge you for the service. When you open a Postbank account, you will also get Girocheques or a *Girobetaalkaart* (Giro card) to use for paying bills.

MEDICAL CARE

The Dutch are the fastest growing and tallest people in Europe. A non-Dutch journalist recently wrote: "In Amsterdam, even at my own height of 6 feet 3 inches, I had to get used to looking up!" Their high protein diet is probably responsible for this but the Netherlands' excellent medical care must play a major role too.

Dutch doctors, nurses and other health workers are conscientious, well-trained and speak English. Hospitals and clinics are modern, well-designed, adequately staffed, and carefully maintained.

Even though the population of the Netherlands is getting older, the average health of the population is still very good. The number of health care facilities has not increased in recent years but there has been an incr°ease in medical expenses. This is caused by higher salaries paid to medical workers and by more use being made of advanced medical equipment.

Paying for Health Care

Fortunately, health care in the Netherlands is still affordable. Like many other major support systems in the Netherlands, the health care system has recently undergone a complete change. In 2006, a new insurance system for curative health care came into force. Under the new Health Insurance Act (*Zorgverzekeringswet*), all residents of the Netherlands are obliged to take out health insurance.

The system is a private health insurance scheme with social conditions and is operated by private health insurance companies. The insurers are obliged to accept every resident in their area of activity. A system of risk equalisation enables the acceptance obligation and prevents direct or indirect risk selection.

The insured pays a nominal premium to the health insurer. Everyone with the same policy will pay the same insurance premium. The Health Insurance Act also provides for an income-related contribution to be paid by the insured. Employers contribute by making a compulsory payment towards the income-related insurance contribution (*collectieve verzekering*) of their employees.

Employers must continue the pay of sick employees for one year. One of the few bits of bad news on the medical front is that there can be a long wait (sometimes months) for routine examinations and other non-urgent medical care.

Get a Family Doctor

A family doctor normally is your first and essential point of contact in the case of physical or mental problems which are not medical emergencies. If necessary, he or she will refer you to a specialist or a hospital. It is therefore important that you find a family doctor and register with him or her as soon as possible after you get to the Netherlands.

Friends or neighbours can advise you on which one to choose. Alternatively, you can look in the *Yellow Pages* under the heading of *Artsen-huiartsen* or in the telephone directory under *huisartsen-(groeps)praktijk*.

AIDS

Deaths from AIDS are decreasing now because people are being more careful and there is a programme to supply drug addicts with clean needles. In Amsterdam, however, AIDS is still the leading cause of death in men between the ages of 30–50.

TELECOMMUNICATIONS

Telecommunications in Holland have taken a great leap forward recently as a result of privatisation, more competition and fewer rules and regulations. There is now much more use of telephones, computers and faxes. More than 90 per cent of the Dutch population of 17 million people now have mobile telephones. In the Netherlands today, having e-mail is a virtual necessity. The number of

Dutch Internet callers rose 17 per cent to over two million in early 2007, resulting in almost total stagnation in the growth of traditional telephony.

Telephones

The public telephone network in the Netherlands is operated by KPN Telecom. You can apply to this firm for phone, fax, Internet and television connections. For mobile telephones, it is best to contact one of the bigger companies, i.e. KPN Telecom, Vodafone, Orange, Telfort, or T-mobile. Because Dutch telephone operators are multilingual, they can easily help foreigners who want to get the number of a person or a company in the Netherlands.

Emergencies

The emergency telephone number in the Netherlands is 112.

By calling it you can contact the police, fire brigade or ambulance service. Be ready to explain what kind of help you need and where it is needed.

One custom in the Netherlands you should be aware of: it is considered good manners to answer the phone by giving your name rather than by simply saying 'hello'.

Telephone Codes

The country code for the Netherlands is 31; the international access code from a Dutch telephone is 00.

The Internet

Virtually all Dutch offices are online. Internet use is highest in business services, wholesale enterprises, banking and insurance, and enterprises selling automobiles or undertaking auto repairs. Companies in hospitality, retail, food, transport and communication, and building sectors are very likely to have their own websites. Most households now have one or more computers. Amsterdam has long billed itself as 'the digital city': via the Internet, you can get access to postal, press and government services. Dutch consumers spent 2.83 billion euros shopping online in 2006, when the number of active online shoppers rose by one million to 6.4 million. Much of their money was spent on travel.

Useful and Popular Website

One of the most popular Dutch sites is:

http:// www.marktplaats.nl

Here you can buy and sell almost anything, from antiques to automobiles. Jobs are advertised on this site too.

Electrical Equipment

Because the Netherlands is on the 220 volt, 50 Hz, three-phase European system, electrical equipment built to American or other standards will require transformers. But even when so equipped, items with electric timing mechanisms or electric motors may not work very well. Audio equipment is notoriously hard to convert. European TV sets and video systems are not compatible with those used in the US.

LEISURE ACTIVITIES

Sports ranks very high on the list of leisure activities. There is no shortage of interesting walks in the Netherlands. Our own favorites include the nature reserves, the beaches and the old sections of Dutch towns and cities. Walking is the most popular recreational activity: 75 per cent of the Dutch go out for walks. Two-thirds of the Dutch take recreational bicycling trips. With almost one-fifth of the country consisting of lakes, canals and rivers, the Netherlands is a paradise for lovers of water sports. Football (soccer), golf, tennis, jogging and squash are very popular too. In the winter, if the ice is thick enough, many people go skating.

Moreover, every city, town or village has at least one sports centre and one indoor swimming pool, provided and maintained by the government. This encourages the Dutch to take part in indoor sports at both recreational and competitive levels.

In winter, waterways turn to ice, providing people of all ages with new opportunities to enjoy the outdoors.

Sports

People between the ages of 36 and 65 are becoming more and more interested in sports, especially in swimming, biking, fitness, football, tennis and golf. But perhaps because of the pressures of school, jobs or having young children, the younger generation (ages 15–35) seems to be getting somewhat less interested in sports.

In any case, as has been suggested earlier, even if you are not very athletically inclined yourself, it is still a good idea for you to join a sports club in order to meet and make friends with Dutch people.

CULTURAL ACTIVITIES

The Dutch have always been keen on cultural activities and sports and love to entertain at home. They will usually be happy to have you join them too.

Today, in order of their popularity, the most common leisure pursuits are: watching TV; meeting friends; participating in

As a leisure activity, reading is less popular these days. Nonetheless, those who still enjoy the printed word are able to find a quiet corner to indulge in their favourite pastime.

games, hobbies, and sports; going out to restaurants or for cultural activities; and reading, which is still popular but is decreasing. Volunteer work, however, is becoming more popular, especially among women.

TV and Films

Even without the addition of a satellite dish, Dutch TV will provide a wide range of programmes in Dutch and other languages. Cable TV brings in a deluge of foreign TV programmes (English, French, Italian, German, Turkish) transmitted in their original languages. Foreign films are shown at local cinemas in their native language with Dutch subtitles (not dubbing) added. The Dutch have gone digital: some 25 per cent of Dutch households now have digital television and 12 per cent use a computer to watch TV.

Plays, Opera, Dance, Music, Museums, Theme Parks

There is never a shortage of cultural activities in the big Dutch cities. Newspapers on Thursdays and Fridays will have information about upcoming events scheduled for the next week. Entertainment guides are also widely available. Tickets can be ordered from box offices at theatres, from VVV offices, and from reservation booking offices. The easiest way to find out what is on offer is to use the Internet. Try the section 'What's on' on http://www.Dutchnews.nl or Google and search for 'What's on' followed by the city of your choice. This way all the information will be in English. Another method is to visit http://www.Holland.com.

VVV has a definitive list of museums in the Netherlands (there are about 1,200 of them and some are among the best in the world). One of the great bargains of cultural life in the Netherlands is the 'museumcard.' At an annual cost of 35 euros, it gives you free access to many of the major museums in the country. The trend among museums seems to be a movement towards mega-exhibits, such as the widely-acclaimed Vermeer exhibition of 1996.

Expatriate and Dutch children (and young-at-heart adults too) will be glad to hear that more and more theme parks are being built in the Netherlands.

ENTERTAINING AT HOME

At one time or another, invitations for morning coffee, drinks before dinner, dinner itself, or for post-dinner-coffee-and-snack are certain to be forthcoming: the Dutch enjoy meeting foreigners and take pride in entertaining them at home. (*See the section* 'Invitations and Good Manners' *in* Chapter 6: Food and Entertaining *on pages 121–123.*)

RELIGION

The Dutch Constitution guarantees freedom of religion. All the major world faiths—Christian, Muslim, Hindu, Jewish etc—are represented in the Netherlands, together with the many different denominations grouped under their banners.

For the last 40 years, organised religion has been declining as a potent force in Dutch life. The Netherlands has the lowest percentage (20 per cent) of churchgoers in Europe. However, 44 per cent of the Dutch say they have a religion.

In the meantime, however, many individual churches, temples and congregations remain quite active. You should therefore have no difficulty in finding one to your liking. In most cases, the services will be conducted in Dutch but there are some English-language services in the major cities.

PETS

Many Dutch keep pets. Dogs are especially popular, as a walk along any city pavement will quickly reveal. Do watch where you put your feet!

There is no quarantine for pets being imported into the Netherlands. For dogs and cats, you will need a valid health certificate (ten days old at the most), stating that the animal has been inoculated against rabies. The certificate, in Dutch, French, German or English, must also give the date of the inoculation, the type of vaccine, a description of the animal and the owner's name.

This document must be endorsed by the official veterinary department of the country of origin (except for Switzerland, Austria and the USA). The animal must have been vaccinated at least 30 days before it crosses the Dutch border. As

AH! THE INTERNATIONAL SIGN OF FRIENDSHIP THE WAGGING TAIL!

regulations frequently change, always check with the nearest Netherlands embassy or consulate.

Dog owners in the Netherlands must pay dog licence fees (*hondenbelasting*). They can apply for a licence by filling out forms obtained from a post office. Failure to do so may result in a fine. EU member states have introduced a new European pet passport for all dogs, cats and ferrets travelling abroad with their owners. These animals are now subject to standardised requirements: an EU pet passport, an identification microchip and a vaccination against rabies.

FOOD AND ENTERTAINING

CHAPTER 6

'A good prince will tax as lightly as possible those commodities which are used by the poorest members of society: grain, bread, beer, wine, clothing, and all other staples without which human life could not exist.'
—Renaissance humanist Desiderius Erasmus

TRADITIONAL FOOD AND DRINK

If it can be said of the French that they 'live to eat', then the Dutch 'eat to live'. Their day does not revolve around food and drink. Just as long as there is enough of everything, the Dutch are likely to be satisfied.

As you can imagine, this very practical, down-to-earth approach to eating has not created one of the world's great cuisines. Instead, Dutch food tends to be unsophisticated, hearty, filling and bland. If you yearn for exotic or spicy flavours, you must do as the Dutch themselves do and go out to an Indonesian or some other kind of ethnic restaurant—of which there are (fortunately) a great many in the Netherlands.

Even if Dutch cooking is never going to shoulder aside French, Italian, Spanish, Chinese or Indian cuisine, it does have its own simple charms. And since you will certainly be introduced to it during your stay in the Netherlands, this is a good time to make our way through the Dutch culinary day.

The food and drink mentioned in this chapter are not only typically Dutch but are also of a high standard: indeed, it is quite above the usual day-in-day-out cooking. So many questions about Dutch food have been posed by foreigners that the editors of the *Windmill Herald*, a bi-weekly Dutch-English newspaper and website, have started an English-language series on traditional Dutch recipes. The website, http://www.godutch.com, introduces you to Dutch recipes in English.

Here we would like to introduce you to the traditional Dutch oven. Ironically, it is better known abroad these days than in the Netherlands. A Dutch oven is a thick-walled cooking pot, usually made of cast iron, with a tightly-fitted lid. It is used in many other countries. In the Australian outback, it is called a camp oven. The French know it as a *cocotte*. The South Africans dub it the *potjie*. By whatever name you call them, Dutch ovens are excellent for slowly simmering roasts, stews, and casseroles.

Breakfast

The Dutch like a cold (uncooked) breakfast. On the well-laden table you may find several kinds of sliced bread (sandwich loaf, rye bread, raisin bread, etc—known collectively as *boterhammen*); butter or margarine, jam and perhaps peanut butter or chocolate flakes (*hagelslag* is a uniquely Dutch topping for bread); two or three kinds of sliced meats (ham, beef or salami); a selection of cheeses, which are to be thinly sliced with a cheese knife; and probably some dry breakfast cereals as well. Everything (except the cereals, of course) is eaten with a knife and fork, not made into a sandwich and eaten with the hands.

A Dutch cheese shop in the city of Zeist. Dutch cheeses are known the world over.

Dutch cheese carriers in the city of Alkmaar.

To drink, there will always be tea or strong filtered coffee (never instant coffee), invariably served with *koffiemelk (*a thick evaporated milk); orange juice or other types of fruit juice; and lots of milk or buttermilk (*karnemelk*) for the children.

A word here about cheese since it is one of the things the Dutch do best. Cheese is never served at the end of a meal but is instead, the real mainstay of breakfast and lunch. Some Dutch people eat a kilogram (2.2 lbs) of cheese a week.

There are many different types of cheese on display in Dutch cheese shops and it is worthwhile to ask the shop attendants about them. Some are semi-creamy when *jonge-kaas* (young cheese) and drier when they are *belegen* or *oude kaas* (mature or old cheese). Edam cheese, shaped into a ball, is as popular in the Netherlands as it is abroad but is often not covered by the well-known red skin. Gouda cheese is wheel-shaped and flat. Other cheeses include *Leidse kaas* (Leiden cheese, flavoured with caraway seeds) and *Friese nagelkaas* (Friesland cheese, flavoured with cloves).

Lunch

Whereas France is famous for the two-hour, wine and dine lunch, in the Netherlands lunch is generally 30 minutes long, usually around 12.30pm.

For the Dutch, lunch is a necessary part of the day in the sense that it's time to refuel for the afternoon's activities. It consists normally of broodjes (soft rolls) filled with meat or cheese and eaten like a sandwich or the Dutch *boterham* (slice of bread) with butter and ham or cheese. Never both. Combinations are usually frowned upon, as they waste filling for another sandwich. If you feel like a warm snack try: an *uitsmijter* (a *boterham* with two fried eggs on top of slices of ham or roast beef), a *broodje kroket* (meat or shrimp croquettes) or chicken *saté* (roast chicken with a delicious peanut sauce either with or without bread). Salads have become very popular as well. Lunch is mostly accompanied by milk, tea, water or soup

Dinner

Dinner is the main meal of the day and is usually served relatively early, between 6:00–7:00 pm. After their light meal at lunch, the Dutch are ready to tuck into some hearty fare in the evening. Because they travel so much and are so internationally minded, they can cook a wide range of European foods, but here are some of the very traditional Dutch dishes you may encounter.

- *Erwtensoep*
  A warming winter green pea soup with sausage, which should be so thick, as the saying goes, that a spoon can stand upright in it.
- *Bruine bonen met spek*
  Brown beans with bacon.
- *Boerenkool met rookworst*
  Mashed potatoes, kale and smoked sausage.
- *Haring* (herring)
  The first herrings of the year (*nieuwe haring*) which are gutted and kept in brine, appear in the spring and are served with chopped onions. When bought from fish stalls on the street, they are traditionally eaten by holding the fish above

one's mouth by the tail and eating it uncooked. The first cask of herrings is ritually offered each year to the queen.

- **Gerookte paling** (smoked eel)
  This is delicious as a starter or a quick snack on the street, where at fish stalls it is put into a *broodje*. In Friesland and North Holland, you may even be invited to a smoked eel party, where the eels are smoked, peeled and then eaten whole.

- **Bitterballen**
  Small meat croquettes, served as an appetiser.

- **Pannenkoeken** (pancakes)
  Sometimes huge, they can be topped by many different kinds of fillings.

- **Vis** (fish)
  Excellent fresh seafood is available in the Netherlands. *Tong* (sole), *schol* (plaice), *tarbot* (turbot), *zeewolf* ('sea wolf') and Zeeland oysters and mussels are good choices.

- **Hutspot**
  Beef stew with potatoes, carrots and onions. This dish dates from 1573, when it was prepared for the starving citizens of Leyden as their first food at the end of the siege of that city.

- **Appelgebak**
  Dutch apple pie, a superb snack or dessert usually served with *slagroom* (whipped cream).

- **Oliebollen** (oil balls)
  Round doughnuts with raisins, dusted with fine sugar, which are a New Year speciality.

Drinks

The Dutch are notoriously fond of strong filtered coffee (*koffie*) served with milk and sugar. Cappuccino is very popular these days. Wine has become more popular. It is not cheap in the Netherlands, however, and is therefore not (as in France) an invariable accompaniment to lunch or dinner.

Dutch beer—of which there is a wide range, differing not only in taste but also in strength—is really excellent. Some traditional alcoholic drinks, however, may be more of an acquired taste. These include *advocaat*, a very thick

**Hertog Jan
Bieren**

Traditioneel Gebrouwen Natuurzuiver

Hertog Jan Beer is just one in the wide range of Dutch beers.

eggnog occasionally enjoyed by ladies after a heavy day of shopping, and several kinds of *jenever* (Dutch gin), which is usually served ice-cold in a small shot glass (*borrel*) filled literally to the brim.

Restaurants

There are more than 1,000 restaurants in Amsterdam alone; other Dutch cities—notably The Hague and Rotterdam—are not far behind. Going out to dinner, whether at a local café or, more rarely, at an expensive restaurant, is a favourite Dutch pastime. You may be invited by Dutch friends. If so, remember that unless the host indicates otherwise, dining out is usually 'Dutch treat', meaning that you will have to pay for your share of the bill.

Rijsttafel Boys

When you tire of the blandness of traditional Dutch food, go find a good *chinees-indisch* (Chinese-Indonesian) restaurant and order an Indonesian *rijsttafel* (rice-table). This is a fabulous meal of rice accompanied by many different side dishes from which you pile spicy helpings of exotic meats, fish, fruits and vegetables, and mix everything together. Dutch beer is, of course, mandatory.

In the past, when colonial officials in the Dutch East Indies sat down to a proper *rijsttafel*, a long line of barefoot 'boys' (waiters) each carried in one of these side dishes—for example, small plates of chicken curry, green pepper, dried fish, coconut, onion, pepper, pineapple, nuts, raisins, bananas and hard-boiled eggs. Once, when the Dutch Governor gave a formal banquet for the Sultan of Yogyakarta (Indonesia), there were 55 'boys' in line!

INVITATIONS AND GOOD MANNERS

Once you have made some Dutch friends, you may be invited to their homes for a coffee, drinks or a meal. Here's what to expect and what you need to keep in mind.

Morning Coffee

If invited to a friend's house for coffee around 10:30 am, you will be offered one *kopje koffie* (cup of coffee) with milk and sugar and one biscuit. When these are finished, you will usually be offered a second cup of coffee, again with one biscuit. After this very Dutch ritual, it is time to take your leave.

Lunch

Invitations for lunch are not as common in the Netherlands as in some other countries. Working people have only a short lunch break and must content themselves with a sandwich or a quick snack; women at home must prepare lunch for their own children. If you do not get invited to lunch, these will probably be the reasons.

Pre-dinner Drinks

Op de borrel or 'come for drinks' is a familiar invitation. This means you should arrive at your friend's house at about 5:30 pm. A choice of wine, beer, *jenever* or sherry may be offered, as well as snacks. Since you have not been invited for dinner, you should leave by about 7:00 pm.

Dinner and Afterwards

The Dutch value their privacy at home and do not extend dinner invitations lightly. Being invited to a Dutch home for dinner is therefore a sign that the host and hostess think well of you and would like to see more of you. For this reason, if for no other, you should be on your best behaviour.

The Dutch eat dinner, the main meal of their day, relatively early. An invitation for 6:30 pm means you are being invited for dinner. You will first be offered a selection of alcoholic and non-alcoholic drinks (the host will tell you what is on offer) together with cheese crackers or snacks and will then be given dinner.

An invitation for 8:00 pm, on the other hand, means only coffee and biscuits, usually followed by drinks and a very light snack. If there is any doubt in your mind about what the hostess has planned, you should telephone her to confirm this is an invitation for coffee.

In any case, whenever you do come it is absolutely essential that you be on time (the Dutch are very punctual) and that you bring a small but good quality present for the hostess—a bunch of flowers or a potted plant (widely available from local florists) are the most common gifts but a little box of chocolates, some decorative candles or a bottle of wine are equally acceptable. But don't overdo it: the Dutch value moderation in all things and bringing an extremely expensive bottle of rare wine would be a bit too much.

The Dutch like to dress informally. Few men wear suits nowadays; grey flannel trousers with a sport coat are much more common and can be worn to dinner. For a more formal dinner at the home of his boss, however, a man might decide to wear a tie as well. To be on the safe side, call beforehand to check.

Children may be present at a family dinner. Even if tempted to do so, do not try to discipline them if they are being noisy or are commenting to each other or to their parents in Dutch about your foreign appearance or strange table manners—this task should be left to the parents.

It is only good manners, of course, to resist any temptation to ask the host or hostess personal questions or to brag about how much you earn or what worldly goods you have. Nor should you criticise the Royal Family. The Dutch are not a flag-waving, highly nationalistic people but they are quietly patriotic nonetheless. Even accurate and well-meant 'constructive' criticism by foreigners may not be appreciated.

Until then, it is best to confine yourself to complaining about the ever-increasing traffic congestion, the frequently terrible weather or the very high taxes.

And just as it is important that you arrive on time, it is important that you be ready to depart on time unless your host and hostess urge you to stay on. Be polite and do not overstay your welcome: be sure to leave when the coffee or liquor refills stop.

WHAT TO SEE AND WHEN TO SEE IT

'Ik kan niet het feit veranderen, dat mijn schilderijen niet verkopen. Maar de tijd zal komen dat mensen zullen erkennen dat zij meer waard zijn, dan de waarde van de verf die ik heb gebruikt in het schilderij.'
('I cannot change the fact that my paintings are not selling, but the time will come when people will recognize that they are worth more than the value of the paint I put on them.')
—Vincent van Gogh (1853–1890)

DESPITE ITS SMALL SIZE, there are plenty of things to see and do in the Netherlands.

MAN-MADE ATTRACTIONS

Over the centuries, the industrious Dutch have created many marvellous things. To reduce this embarrassment of riches to a manageable size, one has to be very selective. Here are some recommendations:

- The major cities of the Randstad: Amsterdam, Rotterdam, The Hague and Utrecht.
- Other attractive cities: Delft, Haarlem, Leiden (this is the Dutch spelling; Leyden is the British spelling), Maastricht and the charming 16th-century fortified town of Bourtange, which is located south-east of the city of Groningen.
- Feats of hydraulic engineering: the Kinderdijk windmills, the Afsluitdijk (Barrier Dam) and the Delta Works.
- Examples of life at opposite ends of the social spectrum: the peat diggings in the province of Overijssel and the royal palace of the House of Orange, known as Het Loo.

MAJOR CITIES OF THE RANDSTAD

If good things come in small packages, the Netherlands certainly qualifies. By world standards, the country's four major cities are really quite small. They are also located very close to each other.

Amsterdam

Most of the nearly 750,000 inhabitants of Amsterdam would assert that their city is the pinnacle of trade, finance and culture in the Netherlands. Indisputably, it is the largest city as well as the capital—but it is not the seat of government, which is The Hague. Built on the banks of two rivers (the IJ and the Amstel), ringed with a network of old canals and dotted with splendid brick homes and world-class museums, Amsterdam is a glorious city.

Smitten by Amsterdam

The authors of this book are both very smitten with Amsterdam. Ria van Eil spent the first 22 years of her life there. Says Ria, "There is no other city like it—it is beautiful, and when you live there you really feel part of it." Hunt Janin and his Dutch wife think that it is, by a wide margin, the most interesting city in the country.

No other city in the world has more tourist attractions within walking distance than Amsterdam. Perhaps this is the reason it hosts 4.6 million foreign visitors each year. Check out Amsterdam's Internet site at:

http://www.amsterdam.nl

But like other European cities, it has a seamy side as well—the well-known 'coffee shops', which openly sell soft

Amsterdam is one of the most attractive cities in the world. As is the case in much of the country, water is a prominent feature.

drugs; a great deal of petty crime (most of it drug-related); and an infamous red-light district, which consists of three or four streets where prostitutes openly display themselves behind red-lighted windows.

Amsterdam's beginnings were modest enough. In 1275, a Count of Holland accorded trading privileges to a little fishing village on the Amstel river built on a *dam* (dyke). The city gradually grew around this village centre, which became Amsterdam's main square, the Dam. In 1610, a central ring of new canals was dug and the Herengracht (the Lords' Canal; *gracht* means canal), the Keizersgracht (Emperor's Canal) and the Prinsengracht (Princes' Canal) became highly desirable building sites for the mansions of newly-rich merchants.

It was in this era—the 17th century, now known as the Golden Age (*more on this later in this chapter on pages 143–149*)—that Amsterdam reached the apogee of its artistic and financial glory.

Rembrandt himself moved from Leiden to Amsterdam in 1630 and died there 39 years later. The Amsterdam stock exchange flourished: paper options on cargoes of spices and other goods shipped from the Netherlands East Indies (now Indonesia) were actively traded, causing the same anxieties the rise and fall of stocks still do more than 350 years later.

The Jewish Lament

In fact, in 1688, when asked whether Dutch stocks would rise or fall, a Jewish merchant of Spanish origin gave an answer which is still timely today. "The shares are shrouded in such a semi-divine haze," he wrote, "that the more he thinks about it, the less he understands; and the more shrewd he is, the more mistakes he makes!"

In any case, the best way to see Amsterdam now is to walk along the Herengracht and other canals, admiring the 17th- and 18th-century homes with the striking gables and façades. Excellent maps and pamphlets and reliable advice can be obtained from the VVV, Netherlands' tourist information centre.

VVV Centres

There are hundreds of VVV centres in the Netherlands, all marked with three blue V's on a white triangle. They are staffed by competent, helpful people who can probably answer any question a visitor is likely to have. VVV centres can be found in all Dutch cities and in many towns as well.

Walks in Amsterdam can also be combined with the popular and outstanding boat tours (Rondvaart), which ply the most important canals. Other not-to-be-missed sights include:

- The Jordaan, Amsterdam's most picturesque neighbourhood, with the photogenic warehouses, homes and quays of the Brouwersgracht (Brewer's Canal).
- The national art museum (Rijksmuseum), a stunning collection of Dutch art, including Rembrandt's celebrated painting of 1642, *The Night Watch*. (A small branch of the Rijksmuseum has been opened at Schiphol Airport, so travellers can admire the works of Rembrandt, van Gogh, and other well-known Dutch painters.)
- The Vincent van Gogh National Museum (Rijksmuseum Vincent van Gogh), where many of his paintings and drawings can be seen.
- The red light districts (Oudezijds Voorburgwal), where you can admire, as your taste dictates, either fine old houses along narrow canals or scantily-dressed ladies sitting invitingly behind curtainless windows.
- The Netherlands Maritime History Museum (Nederlands Scheepvaart Museum) in the city's port, where you can board the ship *Amsterdam*, a full-size (157-foot-/48-m-long), beautifully maintained replica of a Dutch East Indiaman of 1749 mounting 42 guns (cannon). This splendid museum is now closed for a major renovation that will last at least through 2009. During this process, the East Indiaman Amsterdam will remain open to the public. It will, however, be towed to the nearby NEMO science centre.

Rotterdam

Located at the mouth of the Rhine, the Maas and their tributaries, Rotterdam (population nearly 590,000) is the Netherlands' second largest city and the point where sea-and river-borne traffic meet and mingle. Originally, it was only a small village on the *dam* (dyke) of the river Rotte and had little to boast of until the great humanist Erasmus was born there in 1466. But in the late 16th and early 17th centuries, the Sea Beggars (Dutch fighters revolting against Spanish rule) built ports at Rotterdam for their own fleet and the city began to grow.

The city was captured by the French in 1794. Its prosperity went into decline but its fortunes picked up again when Belgium and the Netherlands split up in 1830 and Rotterdam again became a transit point for river traffic. The 19th century witnessed a rapid development of the city and the port.

During World War II, Rotterdam was heavily bombed, first by the Germans in 1940 and then by the Allies in 1943. It was then sabotaged by the retreating Germans in 1944. But after the war, thanks to the industriousness of the Rotterdammers, the city arose from the ashes and is now the world's largest port in terms of tonnage handled, moving hundreds of million tonnes of cargo each year. If you like ships and quays, the best thing to do in Rotterdam is to take one of the SPIDO company's extremely interesting boat tours of this huge port.

Internet Sites for Rotterdam

Check out the Internet site:

http://www.rotterdam.nl

which is available both in Dutch and English, for general information for new residents. It is also a good place to go for hyperlinks to many other English-language Internet sites dealing with Rotterdam.

The Hague

Officially named 's-Gravenhage (literally, 'the country's hedge'), but commonly known in Dutch as Den Haag and in English as The Hague (population just over 475,000 inhabitants), this pleasantly aristocratic and bureaucratic city is the seat of the Netherlands' government, its parliament and many foreign embassies and missions.

Internet Site

Check out this attractive Internet site (in English) for The Hague:

http://www.denhaag.nl

The Hague is also the seat of the International Court of Justice and the site of many international peace conferences. The new International Criminal Court was established here in 2002.

Originally nothing more than a hunting lodge set in a dense forest, The Hague's rise began in about 1250 when the Count of Holland chose it as the site for a castle. A later Count moved his court there at the end of the 14th century. The Hague was pillaged by Dutch mercenaries in 1528 but in the 17th century, it became the seat of the Dutch government and an important diplomatic centre.

The Hague is the seat of Dutch government.

Located in The Hague, the Mauritshuis is one of the finest art museums in the world

In the 17th and 18th centuries, rich merchants built their mansions near the Binnenhof (its name means 'inner courtyard')—the medieval heart of the city—and in the 19th century, many Dutch colonial families returned from Indonesia to settle in The Hague. Queen Beatrix also chose to live in The Hague after her coronation in 1980. Royal Dutch Shell, the oil giant, is headquartered here as well.

In the Binnenhof area are located the First Chamber of Parliament, which is similar to the British House of Lords or the US Senate; the Second Chamber, similar to the British House of Commons or the US House of Representatives; the Ministry of General Affairs; and part of the State Council. The Knights' Hall (Ridderzaal) dates from 1280. Every year on Prinsjesdag (the third Tuesday in September), the Queen, arriving in a golden coach, comes here to outline to the two Chambers the government's plans for the year.

Other worthwhile sights in The Hague are:

- The Royal Picture Gallery (Mauritshuis), one of the most beautiful classic buildings in the Netherlands, with fine paintings by Rubens, Rembrandt and Vermeer.
- The seaside resort of Scheveningen, which has a long sand beach well suited to sunbathing and—for those who

The Oude Gracht runs through the centre of Utrecht city. The canals are bordered with charming restaurants from where you can sit and watch the world go by.

can endure the cold water of the North Sea—swimming as well. There is also a casino and a long pier with a tall observation tower. Scheveningen's most attractive feature to us, however, is the nearby Oostduinpark (East Dune Park). Here, you can enjoy excellent walks, both along the beach itself and the Wassenaarse Slag, and inland behind the big sand dunes protecting the coast. Moreover, there is also a short but lovely road through the dunes to the estate of Meyendel. Only bikers and hikers can use this 4.8-km (3-mile) road.

Utrecht

Still known for its university, which was established in 1636 and is now the largest in the Netherlands, Utrecht (population over 280,000) is at a crossroad for Dutch railways because it is located near the middle of the Netherlands. Everyday over 1,500 trains pass through the city, making the town an important business and trade fair centre.

Utrecht was founded by the Romans in the 1st century AD; they called it Trajectum (meaning 'ford'), from which it gets its present name. A powerful bishopric was based here in medieval times with the blessing of the German emperors. The city is still the seat of Roman Catholicism in the Netherlands. Here, under the terms of the Union of Utrecht (1579), the seven northern provinces formed a united front against Spain. The Treaty of Utrecht (1713) curbed the imperial ambitions of France and ended the Spanish War of Succession. In the 19th century, the city's old ramparts were replaced by parks and many new residential and commercial districts have sprung up since then.

Laced with bridges, the narrow Oude Gracht (old canal) and Nieuwe Gracht (new canal) run through the centre of the city and are bordered by charming restaurants from which you can watch the passing boats. Rising 122 m (370 ft) into the air, the 14th century Dom Tower (Domtoren) is the tallest in the country and one of the most beautiful. St Peter's Church (Pieterskerk), shaped like a cross, dates from 1048. The best collection of medieval art in the Netherlands is in Utrecht's Carathijneconvent Museum.

OTHER ATTRACTIVE CITIES
Delft

Dating from 1100, Delft (the name means 'moat') is the burial place of Prince William of Orange (1533–1584), whom the Dutch revere as the father of their country. Delft was also the home of Hugo de Groot (1583–1645), the father of international law who was better known as Grotius, and of the artist Johannes Vermeer (1632–1675). The blue-and-white earthenware known as Delftware, inspired by Chinese porcelain, has been famous since the 17th century and is still being made today.

This beautiful city should be seen on foot. A walk through Delft will reveal leafy canals, old churches, charming alleys and bridges, and cool interiors suffused with a soft light from sky and water.

Haarlem

The residence of the Counts of Holland, Haarlem was founded in the 10th century. The painter Frans Hals moved here in 1591. This city is now the heart of the tulip industry. Because storms on Haarlem Lake (the Haarlemmermeer) endangered Amsterdam and Leiden, the lake was drained in 1852. It became a productive settled region and, much later, the site of Schiphol Airport. Local attractions include the Frans Hals Museum, the 15th century Great Church (Grote of St Bavokerk) and its adjacent Great Square (Grote Markt), and the 14th century Town Hall (Stadhuis).

Leiden

Leiden is famous for its university, founded in 1575 and the first in the Netherlands. Rembrandt was a student here in 1620. This city is also remembered as a refuge for Protestants fearing persecution in their native countries.

Leiden's attractions now include a lovely old canal (Rapenburg) as well as the last windmill (Molen) built in the city in 1743 and used for milling grain. There are also five museums which highlight, respectively, ethnology, decorative arts, ancient civilisations, geology, scientific instruments and the Pilgrim Fathers.

The city of Haarlem is the centre of the tulip industry in the Netherlands.

The Pilgrims

In 1609, a group of Protestants, known as Puritans or Pilgrims, moved from England, first to Amsterdam and later to Leiden. Eventually, they decided to settle permanently in North America. So, after returning to England, they boarded the good ship Mayflower at the port of Plymouth and in 1620, upon reaching the coast of Cape Cod in what is now the state of Massachusetts, they set up Plymouth Colony, the first permanent settlement in New England.

There they governed themselves under a compact they had drawn up while still at sea. The great freedom they had experienced while in Amsterdam and Leiden found full expression in this 'Mayflower Compact', which was the first constitution of the New World. Americans today still celebrate the Pilgrims' achievements on Thanksgiving Day.

Maastricht

Founded by the Romans at the site where they bridged the river Maas, this city is a major industrial centre with a beautiful old section. St Servatius' Basilica (St Servaasbasiliek) was built around AD 1000 on the site of a sanctuary then four centuries old. The Basilica of Our Lady (Onze Lieve Vrouwebasiliek) was already in place by AD 1000. The city's defensive walls (Walmuur) are highlighted by towers, trees and beautiful gardens. A Dutch friend claims that Maastricht, now up-scale and with hundreds of pubs, is 'the coziest city' in the Netherlands.

FEATS OF HYDRAULIC ENGINEERING
The Kinderdijk Windmills

Dutch windmills fall into two general categories:

- polder mills, designed to lift water
- industrial mills, which sawed timber, husked barley and processed the raw materials needed to grind wheat, make tobacco snuff , ropes, leather, spices and textiles.

Windmills were the most powerful machinery of their day, not playthings, and could generate up to 100 horsepower. By varying the positions of their sails (blades), messages could also be sent. In fact, this was even done during World War II to signal British and American pilots flying over the Netherlands.

Because of their attractiveness, size and number, the 18 polder mills of Kinderdijk (Children's Dyke) are well

A polder mill that is used to lift water and drain the land.

worth visiting. Dating from 1738, they were initially used to drain a marshy plain. They are now illuminated at night for a week in September. One of these windmills (appropriately named De Blokker—'dedicated worker') is open to the public in the spring, summer and early autumn. In July and August, all 18 mills are set in motion every Saturday and sometimes other days as well. In 1997, these famous mills were put on UNESCO's World Heritage List. Visit http://www.kinderdijk.nl.

The Barrier Dam

Built between 1927 and 1932, the barrier dam (the Afsluitdijk) is 30.5 km (19 miles) long and nearly 90 m (295 ft) wide at sea level. It tamed the Zuiderzee by transforming its southern half into a big lake now known as the IJsselmeer (pronounced Eye-ssel-mar).

The most painless way to cross the Barrier Dam is of course by car, but a more challenging way—and the best way to appreciate what the Dutch have accomplished over such a vast stretch of turbulent water—is to ride a bicycle across it. A separate bike lane makes this safe to do at any time, but unless you have good gears and strong legs, a relatively windless day will prove best.

There are four good reasons to take a bicycle tour over the Barrier Dam and the IJsselmeer:

- To learn about traditional Dutch life and culture in this very rural area.
- To understand the nature of reclamation, dykes, and polders, i.e. the Netherlands' endless struggle with the sea.
- To enjoy the sparklingly clean and charming towns, with their row of houses along the streets. Window curtains will be open, so you can look into their spotless interiors and see interesting assortments of furniture and traditional objects.
- To see boats, windmills, a monastery, a castle, a historical museum and art galleries.

There is a sharp contrast in feeling between the countryside in the more built up areas of the Netherlands and the more open lands around the IJsselmeer. Historic towns well

A restored peat digger's house in the province of Overijssel. The long roof is to keep out the prevailing winds.

worth a visit include Marken, Volendam, Hoorn, Enkhuizen, Bolsward, Sloten, Urk and Muiden.

The Delta Works

More than 3 km (2 miles) long and built on two man-made islands, the Eastern Scheldt Dam (Oosterscheldedam) is open to automobile traffic except when there are very high winds. A visit to Delta Expo, an exhibition centre on one of the islands, is worthwhile. It offers not only graphic displays but also a boat trip showing how the Delta Works protect the southern part of the Netherlands from the tides and storms of the North Sea.

LIFE AT OPPOSITE ENDS OF THE SOCIAL SPECTRUM

The Peat Diggings of Overijssel

Part of the province of Overijssel is laced with small canals built for carrying peat and studded with shallow lakes formed when water flooded into the abandoned peat digging. For example, the carefully restored and now postcard-perfect thatched-roof village of Giethoorn—named for the wild goat horns (*geitenhoorns*) once found there—owes its existence to the wet, cold, strenuous and badly-paid business of digging peat by hand in centuries past.

Today, Giethoorn's reed-covered islands are still the source of the thick thatch that is used for its homes and barns. These picturesque barns, with their *kameeldak* (literally, 'camel-roof', meaning 'curved') roofs, are accessible only by water on flat-bottomed punts. The whole village is off-limits to cars but can easily be explored on foot, or even better, by boat. But try to avoid the summer holiday season, when the charm of the village can be marred by swarms of visitors.

The Royal Palace of Het Loo

A keen sportsman, William III, the Prince of Orange, began work on Het Loo Palace (its name means 'an open area in a forest') in 1685 as a hunting estate and a home for his court. Since then, the palace has had a distinguished history in an elegant world far removed from that of the hoary-handed peat diggers.

Enlarged in 1692, Het Loo was captured by the French in 1795, was visited by Napoleon in 1811, became a summer residence for King William I in 1815 and was the home of Queen Wilhelmina after she abdicated in 1948. In 1969, Queen Juliana gave the palace to the nation and following extensive restoration work on the palace itself and its 1,626 acres of land and gardens, it was opened as a national museum (Rijksmuseum Paleis Het Loo) in 1984—almost precisely 300 years after the first spade full of earth was turned for its construction.

Het Loo can be visited year-round but, like many other outdoor sights in the Netherlands, it will be at its best on a sunny summer day.

NATURAL ATTRACTIONS

There is virtually nothing in this tiny country which has not been shaped in one way or another by human hands, so the word 'natural' must be interpreted very loosely. With this caveat in mind, three natural attractions can be recommended: the De Hoge Veluwe National Park (which is also the site of the Kroller-Müller National Museum), the Wadden Islands and the bulbfields.

De Hoge Veluwe National Park

Located between Apeldoorn and Arnhem, this 5,500 hectare (13,338 acre) park consists of beech, oak, pine and birch trees set off by heaths, sand dunes and lakes. It is home to hundreds of deer (red and roe), moufflon (wild sheep), wild boar, foxes, rabbits, badgers and many species of birds. The best time to look for some of these creatures is late afternoon in the winter and spring. The park is open all year round. Visitors can tour the park on the *witte fietsen* (white bicycles) provided free of charge.

This park is also the site of the Kroller-Müller National Museum, which houses paintings by van Gogh, Mondriaan, French Impressionists as well as the Dutch artists of the Golden Age. Contemporary sculpture is on display as well.

Wadden Islands

Lying in an arc north-west of Friesland, the Wadden Islands have fine beaches of white sand, backed by high dunes.

Hyacinth fields that seem to go on forever.

This is a very windy region which is most agreeable on sunny summer days. Texel, 24 km (15 miles) long and 9 km (5.5 miles) wide, is the biggest island and has three nature reserves.

Since driving is not permitted on some of the islands, cycling and walking are the best ways to get around. The Waddenzee is so shallow that at low tide it can actually be crossed on foot; but the unique Dutch sport of *wadlopen* (mud-walking) can only be undertaken with a guide and never in winter.

Low tide uncovers vast areas of mud or sand (*wadden*) which are ideal feeding grounds for resident gulls and ducks. Many migratory birds feed and winter here too, while seals bask on the sand banks off the North Sea coasts of the islands.

The Bulbfields

Introduced from Turkey at the end of the 16th century, tulips have been grown with great success in the fields between Haarlem and Leiden.

The 'great tulip mania' occurred in the 1630s when these flowers were in such demand throughout northern Europe that the Dutch threw their normal caution to the wind and feverishly began buying and selling bulbs purely on a speculative basis. Prices soared; at a time when a skilled worker was earning only 2.8 guilders a week, the rarest bulbs were changing hands at 6,000 guilders each.

The inevitable crash came in 1637 and provoked endless moralising about the evils of speculation, which was denounced as undermining the proper Calvinist relationship between hard work and a good income.

Today, the bulbfields cover more than 21,853 hectares (54,000 acres) and produce 80 per cent of the world's production—about 10 billion bulbs each year. These are best seen in all their glory in the spring, from mid-April until the end of May. This floral checker-board of vibrant colours can be seen by car, train, even from a plane taking off or landing in the Netherlands or from the windmill at the Keukenhof (the National Flower Exhibition), where every year six million tulips, daffodils and hyacinths are planted across its 32 hectares (nearly 80 acres).

DUTCH CULTURE
The Golden Age and Afterwards

The Netherlands has one of the richest cultures in the whole of Western Europe. Since a great deal has already been written about it in English and other languages (especially in the field of art history), we will be very selective and focus on only two of its many aspects:

- The Dutch language itself—both oral and body language—which we shall look at in the next chapter on page 152.
- The arts: painting, music, architecture and design, literature, theatre, dance and the festivals celebrating them.

Pillarisation

The remarkable decline of 'pillarisation'—which had played such an important role in Dutch daily life—during this time also played a major role in contributing to the Golden Age of the Netherlands. (*This has been covered in the section* 'Decline of Pillarisation' *found in* Chapter 2: Overview of Land and History *on pages 27–28.*)

THE ARTS
Painting

The Dutch take justifiable pride in what historians refer to as their 'art mountain', much of which can be admired in the museums of Amsterdam, The Hague, Leiden, Utrecht, Haarlem and Rotterdam. Each artistic period, however, saw so many gifted painters at work that to reduce this embarrassment of riches to manageable size, let us confine ourselves to only six artists. (If no museum is listed after a given painting, this means the work is no longer in the Netherlands.)

A 16th-Century 'Primitive'

- **Hieronymus Bosch** (c 1450–1516) has been described by art historians as 'the most creative painter of fantasy who has lived'. Bosch's best-known paintings include detailed and often grotesque pictures (*Hell, Ship of Fools*), works of pure fantasy (*Adoration of the Magi*) and paintings characterised by detached observation (*The Prodigal Son* found in the Boymans van Beuningen Museum, Rotterdam).

Painters of the Golden Age (17th Century)

- **Rembrandt van Rijn** (1606–1669) achieved great fame as a portraitist who could solve problems of light and shadow, as in *The Anatomy lesson of Dr Tulp* (in the Mauritshuis, The Hague). This shows a group of doctors, dressed chiefly in black, peering intently at the very pale cadaver being dissected before them. At the other end of the human spectrum, however, the warmth, love and tenderness

M.C. Escher
A permanent collection of Holland's most famous graphic artist can seen at 'Escher in the Palace', The Hague. Website: http://www.escherinhetpaleis.nl

of a good marriage are nearly palpable in *Jewish Bride* (in the Rijksmuseum, Amsterdam). The best known of Rembrandt's portraits, however, is certainly *The Night Watch* (also in the Rijksmuseum, Amsterdam), a huge painting showing the officers of the civic guard.

- **Frans Hals** (c 1580–1666) vividly captured the stolid, no-nonsense, enduring qualities of Dutch gentlemen and ladies. Good examples of his work are *Portrait of Nicolaes Woutersz van der Meer* and *Cornelia Claesdr Vooght* (both in the Frans Halsmuseum, Haarlem) as well as the big-sky feeling of the Netherlands itself—*Duinlandschap met konijnenjacht (Dune Landscape With Rabbit-shooting)*—which is also in the Frans Halsmuseum in Haarlem.
- **Johannes Vermeer** (1632–1675) is the master of muted light. What is arguably his finest work, *View of Delft* (in the Mauritshuis, The Hague), shows the city of Delft steeped in a soft golden light reflected from sky, clouds and water. On a more intimate scale, *Girl Reading* conveys a gentle luminous serenity.

19th and 20th Centuries

- **Vincent van Gogh** (1853–1890), it is said, so despaired of foreigners ever being able to pronounce his last name correctly (it sounds something like *van Khokh*) that he signed his pictures with his first name alone. During one of his fits of insanity, he cut off part of his own ear. But van Gogh's bright pigments, inspired by the colours of southern France (*Cornfield* and *Cypress Trees*), and his tortured *Self Portrait* have earned him a lasting place in modern art.

- **Piet Mondriaan** (1872–1944) was a founding member of the abstract art movement known as *De Stijl* (literally, 'the style'), which was centred in the Netherlands. The works of his mature period offer the viewer a carefully calculated selection of cool, pure geometrical shapes. For example, Mondriaan's 1929 *Composition with Red, Yellow, and Blue* (in the Gemeentemuseum, The Hague) is a square white canvas divided by bold black lines into a central white square flanked and balanced by three small red, yellow and blue rectangles.

Music

Music has always been important to the Dutch. Indeed, the most famous organist and composer of the Oude Kerk (Old Church) in Amsterdam, Jan Pieterszoon Sweelinck (1562–1621), was a forerunner of Johann Sebastian Bach. Later Dutch achievements have been more along the lines of performing great music rather than actually creating it. Thus today, the Royal Concertgebouw Orchestra in Amsterdam and the Residentie Orchestra in The Hague are two of the finest ensembles in the world. Opera flourishes in Amsterdam's Muziektheater.

Music is also widely available at less classical levels. Pop festivals are staged throughout the year in the Netherlands. The annual North Sea Jazz Festival in Rotterdam is always well-attended. And last but not least, Saturday shoppers in many Dutch cities can enjoy the rollicking tunes of the ornately decorated street organs, which are nearly identical to their 19th century predecessors and which are played on the street by itinerant musicians who will welcome a bit of your loose change.

Architecture and Design

The solidly constructed and beautifully maintained 17th and 18th century houses lining the canals of major cities are architectural masterpieces still in daily use as offices and elegant private homes. In the 20th century, Dutch architects turned their attention to urban development (chiefly in Amsterdam and Rotterdam), new towns (Almere and Zeewolde), rapidly growing areas (Zoetermeer) and official buildings (the long, low, modernist headquarters of the Dutch Institute for Architecture and Town Planning in Rotterdam).

The best known force in Dutch design was the Spartan, rigorously geometric De Stijl movement, a group of designers and artists who flourished in the 1920s. A classic example of their work is Gerrit Rietveld's famous armchair, which is now in Utrecht's Centraal Museum.

Literature

Dutch contributions to world literature seem to have been greater in the past than in more recent times. In the Middle Ages, for example, Dutch writers produced (in Latin) Arthurian romances and animal allegories which are part of the fabric of Western European tradition. Erasmus' great 16th century work, *In Praise of Folly*, was widely translated. The Golden Age of the 17th century saw many Dutch writers at work and the 1637 publication of the authorised Dutch version of the Bible helped to solidify the Dutch language itself. The biggest book market in Europe is held on a Sunday in early August in the historical town of Deventer. It is known for the quality, quantity and variety of books sold there. This is a unique event with a wonderful atmosphere.

Subsequently, however, most Dutch writers, no matter how talented and well-known in their own country, could not attract a wider circle of non-Dutch readers because of the language barrier. Two major 19th century novelists, for example, were not easily accessible to foreign readers for a long time.

The first of these is Eduard Douwes Dekker (best known under his pseudonym, Multatuli, and for his book *Max Havelaar*), who heaped scorn upon Dutch colonial rule in what is now Indonesia. The other novelist is Louis Couperus, who dissected the bourgeois society of The Hague and who in *The Hidden Force* also wrote about the futility of the Dutch colonial enterprise.

A few modern Dutch writers, such as the historian Johan Huizinga (*The Waning of the Middle Ages*), have been widely translated but most of the post-World War II generation of Dutch novelists have not. As a result, few if any well-read British or American readers are familiar with them.

But thanks to the efforts of the Association for the Production and Translation of Dutch Literature, more Dutch literary works are being translated into other languages. Now that this process is picking up speed, modern Dutch writers may at last become better known abroad. Examples of these authors are: Hermans, Mulisch, van het Reve, Haasse, Wolkers, Nooteboom, 't Hart and van der Heijden.

Theatre

Since professional theatre companies in the Netherlands get part of their funding from the government, they can afford to offer a varied repertoire. There are many smaller companies too, some of which also get government support. They try to create new forms of theatre by bringing together music, mime and new media techniques. But since most theatre companies perform in Dutch, their appeal to foreigners is limited.

Dance

There are major dance companies in, respectively, Amsterdam (the National Ballet), The Hague (the Netherlands Dance Theatre) and Rotterdam (the Scapino Ballet). The National Ballet specialises in classical ballets, while the other two companies perform more contemporary works. The many smaller dance companies, for their part, offer productions of modern dance.

Trams along Leidsestraat. Netherlands has an efficient transport system and it is easy to get around most parts of the country.

Winter fun: families enjoy a day of ice skating.
Rijksmuseum is in the background.

The residential streets in Amsterdam are quiet and pretty and free from noisy traffic. Amsterdam is one of the most bicycle-friendly cities in the world and many people cycle to get around.

The Stock Exchange in Amsterdam. It merged in 2000 with the Brussels Stock Exchange and the Paris Stock Exchange to form Euronext.

A street stall selling clogs and tulips, which are popular with tourists as the country is well known for them.

Artistic Festivals

The Holland Festival, held throughout the month of June, is the most prominent annual festival and has a broad international programme. Medieval and Baroque music are the highlights of the Holland Music Festival, held in Utrecht. The Theater Festival, held jointly in The Hague and Antwerp (Belgium), offers Dutch and Flemish stage productions.

The Holland Dance Festival is held in The Hague. And to complement the Netherlands' own film industry (which has made some excellent documentaries), the Rotterdam Film Festival is held each year. A Poetry International festival is held annually in Rotterdam.

CALENDAR OF FESTIVALS AND HOLIDAYS

When no dates are given, this means the holiday or celebration is held on a varying schedule.

- **31 December–1 January**
  New Year's Eve is celebrated with loud firecrackers and fireworks before, at and after midnight. One of the most traditional foods of this season is *oliebollen* ('oil balls'— round sugared donuts filled with raisins). New Year's Day is a public holiday.

- **March/April**
  Some shops and offices close on Good Friday. Easter Monday is a public holiday.

- **30 April**
  Koninginnedag, the birthday of Queen Juliana, is celebrated as the Queen's official birthday and is a public holiday. Queen Beatrix goes to one or two towns on this festive occasion and is greeted with parades, flags and music.

- **4 May**
  Memorial Day commemorates those who died in World War II. It is not an official holiday but at 8:00 pm, two minutes of silence are observed.

- **5 May**
  Liberation Day celebrates the liberation of the Netherlands by Allied armies in 1945.

- **May**
  Ascension Day is a public holiday.

- **May/June**
  Whit Monday is a public holiday.
- **First Saturday of June**
  Vlaggetjesdag (Flag Day), which officially welcomes the first catch of herring of the season, is held at the harbour of Scheveningen. Vlaggetjesdag refers to the little flags (*vlaggetjes*) with which the ships are dressed.
- **Mid-June**
  Oerol Festival on the island of Terschelling, off the north coast of the Netherlands, features avant garde theatre, dance, art and music.
- **Early July**
  The North Sea Jazz Festival is world-renowned and is one of the highlights of the European cultural season.
- **July**
  Four-Days Marches (Vierdaagse)—Known as the largest scheduled civilian walking event in the world. Each year tens of thousands of people take part, coming from all over the world to hike through Nijmegen's beautiful countryside.
- **Early August**
  The biggest book market in Europe is held on a Sunday in early August in the historical town of Deventer.
- **September**
  The third Tuesday of September is *Prinsjesdag* (Prince's Day), when the Queen, arriving majestically in her golden coach, officially opens the next session of Parliament.
- **5 December**
  Sinterklaas celebrations in the evening (see the following section for more details).
- **25–26 December**
  Christmas Day and Boxing Day are both public holidays. In the past, no major presents were given on Christmas Day. Instead, families and friends met for lunch or dinner and went to church together. Gradually, however, the Dutch are beginning to follow the tradition of giving each other presents on Christmas Day, rather than at the Sinterklaas celebration on 5 December.

Sinterklaas and Christmas

In December, the Dutch celebrate not only Christmas (25 December) but also St Nicholas Day (5 December) as well. This is the day when good children get presents.

All Dutch children and adults know that every year, Sinterklaas (St Nicholas) comes to the Netherlands from Spain by ship, arriving in Amsterdam. He is always riding a white horse and is dressed as a bishop because he is supposed to be the Bishop of Myra (Turkey), the patron saint of children, young women, and sailors.

One or two naughty servants known as Zwarte Piet (Black Peter) always come with St Nicholas and carry canes with which to punish children who have done wrong. The discovery of *pepernoten* (round biscuits made of gingerbread) in the house is clear proof that Zwarte Piet has been there.

Several days before St Nicholas Day, Dutch children put a shoe by the fireplace so that Sinterklaas can leave a small present in it. On the evening of 5 December, presents are given to adults and children alike, often accompanied by short humorous poems on family themes.

This is also the time to eat such traditional delicacies as *borstplaat* and *speculaas* (different kinds of sweets), *taai-taai* (biscuits and cakes in various shapes and sizes) and *boterletters* or *chocoladeletters* (letters of the alphabet created from almond paste or chocolate).

Dutch settlers brought many of these customs to Nieuw Amsterdam (now New York) in the 17th century. Over the years, their own Sinterklaas gradually evolved into the Santa Claus who is so familiar in the world today.

THE DUTCH LANGUAGE

'Adept traders though they be, the Dutch have found it hard to export their language. Its guttural 'g' has potential clients muttering about diseases of the throat, and foreign lips and tongues give out entirely when trying to wrap themselves around 'ui'... Historically, Dutch is related to German...[but] it is a softer, comfier, muddier tongue that seems to have grown up out of the bogs and polders...'
—Rodney Bolt, *A Xenophobe's Guide to the Dutch*, 1995.

MORE THAN 21 MILLION DUTCH and Flemish (Belgian) people speak Dutch, a Germanic language with many parallels with German and English. There are also Dutch speakers in north-west France and it is the language of education and government in the Netherlands Antilles, Aruba and Suriname. Because Indonesia was once a colony of the Netherlands, some senior Indonesian lawyers, officers and historians can speak it too. And one of the languages of South Africa—Afrikaans—originates from the Dutch spoken in the 17th century.

Dutch, however, is not the only official language of the Netherlands; in the northern province of Friesland, Frisian is the mother tongue of nearly 650,000 Frisians. It is not a dialect of Dutch but a separate, though similar, language.

Unlike British English—in which even to the untutored ear of the foreigner, one kind of accent is clearly upper class and another is clearly working class—the Dutch language reflects social differences more subtly. Although the Netherlands today is overwhelmingly a middle class society and becoming more so all the time, there is nevertheless a well established and prosperous 'old' upper middle class.

Much less visible is the Dutch aristocracy, which consists of 150–200 families with a total of 10,000 members. It is certainly in keeping with the Dutch tradition of social equality, however, that being an aristocrat does not mean very much, either to the public at large or to the aristocrats themselves.

Dutch names on the door bell to an apartment.

These upper middle class and aristocratic Dutch men and women can be detected not so much by their worldly goods (they definitely do not believe in conspicuous consumption) but by the more refined Dutch they speak. Only a native speaker of Dutch, however, is likely to notice the slight differences in their speech.

For a foreigner, being able to read some Dutch is very useful indeed—for menus, shopping, newspaper headlines, road signs and travel by train, tram, bus or bicycle—but if you will be in the Netherlands for only a year or two, are not looking for a job and can make yourself understood in

English, German or French, you will not actually need to speak much Dutch.

The more you know, the better, of course. For those with the time and aptitude, learning Dutch is certainly a good idea and will make your stay in the Netherlands easier and more enjoyable.

On the other hand, if you are looking for a job with a Dutch firm, the ability to speak and read Dutch may well be a requirement. (Because English is so widely used in the Netherlands, proficiency in English is not a sought-after skill and as such will not be very helpful in a job search.) Fortunately, there are many schools and individuals in the Netherlands which are well-qualified to teach Dutch.

But be warned: as soon as they perceive you are a foreigner, the Dutch are very likely to address you in any language except Dutch. They take pride in showing off their knowledge of other languages and unless you can make really exceptional progress in mastering their own language—which is not a terribly easy one for most foreigners because of its guttural sounds and long words, as in *tewerkstellingsvergunning* (an employment permit)—the Dutch will probably want to communicate with you in English, German, French or whatever other language they suppose you speak best.

A mural in Dutch for a barber shop.

Pronunciation Guide

Vowels

- **a**   as *a* in *hard* but shorter OR

  as *a* in *cat* but longer
- **e**   as *e* in *set* but shorter OR

  as *a* in *lane*
- **i**   as *i* in *bit*, but shorter
- **o**   as *o* in *hot* but shorter OR

  as *oa* in *boat*
- **u**   as *u* in *hurt* but shorter OR

  as *oo* in *boot*, said with pursed lips
- **eu**   as *u* in *hurt*, said with tightly rounded lips
- **oe**   as *oo* in *book*, said with rounded lips
- **ie**   as *ea* in *cheat*

Consonants

- **b**   as *b* in *boy*
- **c**   as *c* in *cat*
- **ch**   as *ch* in the *loch*
- **d**   as *d* in *dog*

  as *t* when at the end of a word
- **f**   as *f* in *fish*
- **g**   as *ch* in *loch*
- **h**   as *h* in *how*
- **j**   as *y* in *yes*
- **k**   as *ck* in *back*, but exhaling less air
- **l**   as *l* in line
- **m**   as *m* in *me*
- **n**   as *n* in *nice*
- **p**   as *p* in *pit*, but exhaling less air
- **r**   as *r* in French
- **s**   as *s* in *sit*
- **sch**   somewhere between *s* in *sit* and *ch* in *loch*
- **t**   as *t* in *tape*
- **v**   as *v* in *give*, but with more of an *f* sound
- **w**   as *w* in *will* but more of a *v* sound, said with the bottom

  teeth up against the top lip
- **z**   as *ds* in pads.

BODY LANGUAGE

Unlike the Italians and some other nationalities, the Dutch do not use body language very much. In the formal portraits by Frans Hals and others, their ancestors are clearly stolid and impassive. The Dutch of today carry themselves in a more relaxed, informal way and are quicker with a smile than a frown, but they still value social restraint.

Perhaps for this reason, the people of the Netherlands have never developed an extensive vocabulary of hand, facial or other gestures. Only four exceptions come to mind:

- In moments of anger, tapping or pointing at the forehead with the index finger shows you think the person in question is mentally unbalanced.
- Tapping the side of the head with the index finger, however, is a way of saying that person is quite intelligent.
- As it is in other countries, a vertical middle finger standing alone, is a highly insulting and obscene gesture.
- Finally, there is the *vermanende vingertje* (wagging index finger) mentioned earlier, which warns against laziness or mischief.

In general, however, when the Dutch wish to communicate, they usually rely on words, not body language.

DOING BUSINESS IN THE NETHERLANDS

CHAPTER 9

'I believe that producing pictures, as I do, is almost
solely a question of wanting so very much to do it well.'
—MC Escher (1898–1972)

JUST AS THE NETHERLANDS IS A GOOD PLACE TO LIVE, it is also a good place to do business. The hard-working Dutch have a long tradition of being successful world traders. Their thriftiness is legendary. As an old saying has it, *op de kleintjes letten* ('watch the little ones')—that is, watch the pennies and the pounds will take care of themselves. Business is still a highly respectable occupation, and so is making money.

In 2006, the Netherlands was the third richest country in the EU (after Luxemburg and Ireland) in terms of gross national product. The average Dutch income is 31 per cent above the EU average. The business climate in the Netherlands ranges from reasonable to good. One problem is that Dutch companies do not invest enough in research and development. Companies also bring relatively few new products into the market and the number of start-ups and fast growing companies is low in comparison with some other highly developed countries. Compared with Britain and the US, for example, there are not many new Dutch enterprises each year. The Dutch have relatively little enthusiasm for entrepreneurship, probably due to the legal and regulatory maze formed by government regulations designed to protect the common good. On the other hand, the Dutch score well in terms of other conditions favouring economic growth, e.g., political and economic stability, low inflation, low long-term interest rates, and low national and state debts.

NO HIDDEN SNAGS

Business in the Netherlands is conducted above board and in a straightforward way. The Dutch put a very high value on integrity, efficiency, directness and honesty. A Dutch business partner—and it is a good idea to have one if you are setting up a sizeable enterprise—is not likely to cheat you. There is virtually no official corruption. The governmental, tax and legal systems of the Netherlands can be complicated and very frustrating, but at least they are not malevolent, on the take, or staffed by incompetent officials.

To be able to take full advantage of the business opportunities available today, it may first be useful to learn a bit about the Dutch economy and workforce, about working in the Netherlands, and about Dutch business manners, taxes, opening hours and holidays.

The information in this chapter will let you hold your own intellectually in any gathering of the Dutch business world. But you will find it has practical applications too, whether you are an employee of a multinational company in Rotterdam or whether you decide to go to work for yourself as a freelance consultant. Most importantly, it may also give you some ideas about where your own talents can best be put to use.

LEARNING ABOUT DUTCH BUSINESS LIFE

The World Trade Institute, which is part of the Beurs-World Trade Centre, in Rotterdam, offers an evening introductory course (in English and for a fee) on Dutch business life. Although the course is primarily designed for foreign entrepreneurs who are setting up a business in the Netherlands, it may interest freelance workers too, because it covers so much useful ground.

The course looks at the organisational structure of the Netherlands: market research and market information, international trade, permits and liability, the financial system of the Netherlands, employees and work contracts, taxation and duty, and living and working in the Rotterdam area. Less ambitious 'customised' courses, tailored to your own specific needs, can also be arranged.

In 2007, the World Trade Centre in Rotterdam won the equivalent of five stars as an outstanding venue for training, international meetings, trade fairs, receptions and other events. The Centre's combination of high quality catering and experienced project managers suggests that its future will be bright.

A Very Useful Source:
The Netherlands Foreign Investment Agency

The Netherlands Foreign Investment Agency (NFIA) is one of the best sources for accurate, up to date information on doing business in the Netherlands. We therefore commend its website (http://www.nfia.com) to you. It explains why foreign companies find the Dutch such good international business partners. For example:

- The Netherlands has a very long history in international trade, going back to the days of the Dutch East India Company, and is still very good at it. Thanks to its central geographical position, excellent accessibility and fine infrastructure, the Netherlands is now well situated for doing business with the EU, central and eastern Europe, the Middle East, Asia and Africa.
- Rotterdam is still ranked as the world's largest seaport; Schiphol Airport is an international business hub. Communications are excellent: the Netherlands is one of the world's most wired countries, thanks to more than a decade of prescient investment in high-speed Internet, cable and digital communications systems.
- Dutch workers are among the most educated, most flexible and most highly motivated workforces in Europe. Dutch professionals are multilingual and well-travelled. Their worldwide experience helps them deal competently with international business matters.
- Within the Netherlands itself, the quality of life is among the highest in the world. Moreover, the costs of living, housing, education and cultural activities are lower than in most other developed European countries.

The NFIA also provides useful information on other important aspects of business life: hiring employees, business laws and taxes, commercial real estate, shipping goods in and out of Europe through the Netherlands, expatriate life in the Netherlands, and links to other organisations and resources.

The Dutch economy is expected to grow robustly—by up to 3 per cent by the end of 2009. If so, the labour market will probably tighten, leading to wage and price rises. This may slow economic growth a bit but, in general, the business outlook is favorable.

An interesting development is that the Netherlands is now looking at what legal obstacles need to be overcome in Dutch banking laws to allow Islamic banks to be set up. Such banks offer banking according to strict *sharia* (Islamic) principles. These principles, which appeal to devout and increasingly prosperous Muslims, do not allow interest to be paid on loans (this is considered *usury*) and do not sanction investments in industries that deal in alcoholic beverages, weapons or pornography.

THE DUTCH WORKFORCE

The president of a foreign computer software company put it in a nutshell. At the upper end of the employment scale, he said, "we found that the Netherlands offers the most sophisticated talent pool in Europe." The high degree of job competence in the Netherlands is largely the result of the country's excellent education system and is perhaps the single most important reason the Dutch economy is performing so well in global competition. According to a British research organisation, Dutch workers are the happiest in their jobs and are much less inclined to complain about their work than workers in Britain and France. Indeed, only 8 per cent of Dutch workers complain that they don't have enough free time.

The Dutch also have the most flexible workforce in Western Europe. There are, for example, about 550,000 'flexiworkers' —men and women who work a variable number of hours or who are on a temporary contract. This means that one out of 12 people in the workforce is a flexiworker. Such a worker is, on the average, 31 years old and works 28 hours a week. Nearly half the flexiworkers are women.

These flexiworkers play a vital role in the Dutch economy by filling temporary gaps in production and service industries. This is important because in the Netherlands, it is extremely difficult for management to fire anyone or to tamper with the regular work week.

But the lot of the flexiworkers is not always an enviable one. Many of them are mothers, school dropouts or immigrants. They have only limited prospects, less security than people on long-term contracts, often no higher education, do not earn much money, have no pension build-up, no early retirement, no additional on-the-job training and no company-financed insurance against illness, disability or unemployment.

Moreover, the Dutch economy is shifting away from heavy industry (which, in any case, is becoming more automated and needs fewer workers) and towards the service industries. There will, therefore, be fewer low-level industrial, commercial and administrative jobs.

Instead, the demand will be for talented, highly-trained men and women—computer programmers, systems analysts, managers, journalists, interpreters, international lawyers, logistics experts, artists—and people in the medical and semi-medical professions.

Highly skilled immigrants are defined as those who come to the Netherlands for employment and earn a gross salary of at least 46,451 euros, or 34,130 euros if they are less than 30 years old. Approximately 8,800 highly skilled foreign nationals have made use of the rapid admittance procedure that was introduced in 2004. Family members of highly skilled immigrants who join the immigrants in the Netherlands at a later date can now obtain a residence permit within two weeks. Foreign students who want to change their study-related status will soon be able to apply for highly skilled immigrant status. This should make it easier for talented foreign nationals to find jobs in the Netherlands.

If you happen to fall into one of these 'in-demand' job categories and if you learn Dutch, you may well be able to find work in the Netherlands. But see below first!

WORKING IN THE NETHERLANDS
Work Permits

EU nationals do not need a Dutch work permit (commonly known as a *werkvergunning*) and can take any job they can get. But if you are not an EU national and if you want to work for a company in the Netherlands, whether as a shop assistant or as the Chief Executive Officer, you will have to get a work permit from the labour exchange (*Arbeidsbureau*) in the city of your proposed employment.

It takes some effort for expatriates to get work permits. The basic problem is that the Dutch will not issue them except to people who have special skills which are neither available in the Netherlands nor in the wider EU workforce. Companies hiring illegal workers face fines of up to 8,000 euros per illegal worker.

The Dutch workforce itself is so well-trained and so flexible that it can usually supply whatever skills are needed. Other problems are that the employer as well as the employee must apply for the work permit, and that many employers want their workers to know Dutch. Furthermore, a foreigner who hopes to be officially transferred to the Netherlands by his or her employer abroad must have worked for that employer for at least one year.

Working in the Netherlands

Excellent Internet sources for detailed information, both in Dutch and in English, about working in the Netherlands are:

http://www.werk.nl

http://www.kvk.nl

Working on Your Own

The good news is that you do not need a work permit to work freelance. So if you have a skill which is in demand, you may be able to become a freelance consultant. Being able to speak and read Dutch will, of course, be an enormous asset but you may be able to get by without this skill if you have a product that is wanted badly enough.

Nor in most cases do you need a work permit to start your own small business. A business permit, however, will probably be needed for entrepreneurs who want to engage in certain endeavours in Rotterdam or other big cities.

Examples of such urban enterprises are: itinerant trade (market and street trade), second-hand trade, retail trade (opening a shop), skilled trades (e.g. house painters), catering and some service companies (e.g. operating a beauty salon).

Otherwise, if there is something you can make and sell yourself, it is easy enough to set up your own business. The main thing you need is a listing with the local Chamber of Commerce (*Kamer van Koophandel*), which is also an excellent source of information on business permits and commercial prospects in general.

Hiring and Firing

If you do set up your own business, however, please be careful before you hire any employees; it is very hard to get rid of them. In theory, instant dismissal can be justified when an employee is truly incompetent, steals from you, grossly neglects his or her duties repeatedly or refuses to follow reasonable instructions. In practice, however, any employee so dismissed will immediately seek legal redress and you may find yourself involved in a long, expensive legal battle.

Childcare

More and more women are now working full-time but the Netherlands still does not offer a newcomer the wide range of childcare facilities that are available in some other countries.

If you have very young children (under the age of five), it may be difficult to find someone to look after them. The majority of mothers attach great importance to paid work; at the same time, half of them believe that it is best for a baby or a toddler to be looked after exclusively by its own parents. So unless you can somehow manage to work out of your own home until the children are old enough to go to school, this can severely limit your employment prospects.

Employment Contracts

Legally, if you work full-time for someone who has the right to give you instructions that you must follow, you are considered to be an employee. This means you will need an employment contract.

Such contracts can be made verbally or in writing but to avoid any possible misunderstandings and legal battles, it is much better to have a formal written contract signed by both the employer and the employee.

Salaries are negotiable and are usually paid each month into your giro or bank account. However, because of the very heavy tax burden (see the next section), your net pay may well be about half of your gross earnings. So other benefits (some of them taxable too) are frequently offered by employers to recruit and keep good employees.

Perhaps you may be able to negotiate some of these 'extras' into your own work contracts: one additional month of pay each year (this is referred to as 'the 13th month'); rewards for high productivity; commissions on sales; profit-sharing arrangements; access to company canteens or social clubs; help with savings, mortgages or pensions; a company car and allowances for business expenses.

TAXES

The high quality of life in the Netherlands has to be paid for somehow and as a result, the Dutch are one of the most heavily-taxed peoples in the world. Tax rates vary with income level and range from a low of 34 per cent to a high of 52 per cent. If you are transferred by your company to the Netherlands or if you work there in some other capacity, you too will be liable to these stiff taxes.

But because the tax picture is always subject to change and is quite complicated (for example, there is a special—and very favourable—expatriate tax status technically known as

the '30 per cent ruling' which may apply to you), it is strongly recommended that you seek qualified tax advice once you are in the Netherlands.

Help with Taxes

Friends or colleagues may well know someone in this business. Tax consultants are also listed in the *Yellow Pages* under the heading *Belasting consulenten/ belasting adviseurs* or in the telephone directory under *belastingadviesburo*.

As a first step, however, a website (http://www.expatica. com) and a booklet from KPMG—all in English—are excellent sources of useful information for business executives and expatriates:

- *Investment in the Netherlands*, This publication is in both English and Chinese—prepared by KPMG as a source of information to answer many questions asked by business executives when they explore prospective locations for their company's activities in Europe or when they have already decided to establish a presence in the Netherlands. Website: http://www.kpmg.nl

BUSINESS MANNERS

The Dutch are direct, open people and not given to Machiavellian intrigues. They will undoubtedly excuse any minor social blunders you may make but just to be on the safe side, here are seven helpful hints on Dutch business etiquette.

- **Be honest and modest.**

  Because the Netherlands scores very highly on comparative scales of international business integrity, it is extremely important that expatriate businessmen and businesswomen be perceived, above all, as being honest. Toward this end, until you can form some clear idea of what the acceptable limits of exaggeration are, you should limit yourself to describing your products and your own achievements only in the most accurate and most modest terms.

- **Don't be too informal.**

  Using someone's first name without being asked to do so is considered very impolite. Business cards are extremely useful to get names and titles right. 'Drs', for example, signifies a university graduate, not a medical doctor or a PhD, which is abbreviated as 'Dr'.

- **Remember that the Dutch are very busy people.**

  Making appointments well in advance of a proposed meeting is essential; turning up uninvited or asking for an appointment on very short notice suggests a lack of consideration. Always be on time and never take up more time than is actually needed to conduct your business.

- **Don't count on working lunches.**

  Most people have only 30 minutes or so in which to have a sandwich or a quick snack for lunch. The long working lunch, replete with food and drink at a good restaurant and hopefully culminating in a deal, is not as common in the Netherlands as is in the US or UK.

- **Don't forget about birthdays.**
  As mentioned in Chapter 4: Dutch Society (*page 75*), birthdays are important events. When it is your own birthday, you must bring cakes to the office so that during a coffee break, your colleagues can celebrate this happy occasion.
- **Finish your business during normal working hours.**
  The official work week is 36 hours and for most people this is enough. A Dutch man or woman usually wants to be home for dinner by about 6:30 pm, which means they have to leave the office relatively early, given the inevitable commute involved. Working business dinners are occasionally arranged, however, either to continue discussions about an unresolved issue or (more likely) to celebrate a deal, but they will rarely begin later than 7:00 pm.
- **Join a business club.**
  In the big Dutch cities, there is no shortage of international and bilateral business clubs, Rotary organisations or international Chambers of Commerce to choose from. By joining one or more of the organisations, you will not only make useful business contacts but will also get a chance to see Dutch business manners in action.

OPENING HOURS

These are normally from 9:00 am–6:00 pm, Mondays to Fridays. On Saturdays, the majority of shops close at 5:00 pm. In most cities, shops are generally open late on Thursdays, i.e. until 9:00 pm. On Monday mornings, shops are often closed until 1:00 pm. In large towns, shops are open on Sundays from 12:00 noon–5:00 pm. In some big cities, a few supermarkets stay open until 8:00 pm or even until 10:00 pm.

Banks are open from 9:00 am–4:00 pm or 5:00 pm, Mondays through Fridays. Post offices are usually open from 8:30 am–5:00 pm (Mondays to Fridays), but a few post offices are open on Saturdays too, from 9:30 am–12:00 noon or 1:00 pm.

Business offices are normally open from 9:00 am– 5:00 pm or 6:00 pm, Mondays through Fridays. Public (e.g. government) offices work more restricted hours. In general, from 9:00 am–12:00 noon, but it is wise to telephone ahead and check

Since most shops are not open 24 hours, seven days a week, it would be a good idea to keep a list (at least, when you first arrive) of the opening hours of the stores in your area. That way, you won't find yourself running out of your favourite food.

Most Dutch towns hold an open-air market once a week. Some drugstores (chemists) will be open on a rotating basis to cover needs arising in the evening, at night and on the weekends. Restaurant hours vary, but restaurants are usually open for lunch from 11:00 am–2:30 pm or 3:00 pm, and for dinner from 5:30 pm–10:00 pm. The Dutch like to eat dinner early, so do not expect to be served if you turn up at 10:00 pm.

THE NETHERLANDS AT A GLANCE

CHAPTER 10

'Most people only get to visit great works of art...
The Dutch get to live in one.'
—KLM Royal Dutch Airlines advertisement, 1988.

COUNTRY STATISTICS
Official Name
Kingdom of the Netherlands

Capital
Amsterdam

Seat of Government
The Hague

Flag
Tri-colour flag of red, white and blue (in that order from top to bottom).

National Anthem
Wilhelmus van Nassouwe (William of Nassau). Better known as *Het Wilhelmus.*

Time
Greenwich Mean Time plus 1 hour (GMT + 0100).

Land
Located in north-western Europe, with Belgium to the south, Germany to the east and the North Sea to the north and west.

The Dutch coat of arms.

Area
Total (land and water): 42,696 sq km (16,485 sq miles)

Highest Point
Drielandenpunt (322 m/1,056 ft), in the southern-most tip of the Netherlands.

Major Rivers
Rhine River, Maas River and Scheldt River

Climate
Temperate weather with cool summers and mild winters

Natural Resources
Arable land, limestone, natural gas, peat, petroleum, salt, sand and gravel

Population
About 17 million

Ethnic Groups
The Dutch make up 90 per cent while the remaining 10 per cent is made up of Moroccans, Turks, Surinamese and others.

Religion

2002 statistics show that the Roman Catholic Church make up 31 per cent, Dutch Reformed Church 13 per cent, Calvinist 7 per cent, Muslim 5.5 per cent and others 2.5 per cent. Forty-one per cent claim no religion whatsoever.

Languages and Dialects

The official language is Dutch and within the province of Friesland, Frisian is an official language.

Government

The Netherlands is a parliamentary democracy with three branches. The first is the Executive, which consists of the monarch (Queen Beatrix), who is head of state; the prime minister, who is head of government; and the cabinet. The second branch is the Legislative, which is a bicameral parliament, composed of the First and Second Chambers. The third branch is the Judicial, headed by the Supreme Court. There are two dependent areas in the Caribbean: Aruba and the Netherlands Antilles.

Administrative Divisions

Twelve *provincies* (*provincie* is the singular):
Drenthe, Flevoland, Friesland (Fryslan), Gelderland, Groningen, Limburg, Noord-Brabant, Noord-Holland, Overijssel, Utrecht, Zeeland, Zuid-Holland
Dependent areas are Aruba and Netherlands Antilles

Currency

Euro (€)

Gross Domestic Product (GDP)

US$ 512 billion (2006 est)

Agricultural Products

Fruits, grains, potatoes, sugar beets, vegetables

Industries

Agro-industries, chemicals, construction, electrical machinery and equipment, fishing, metal and engineering products, microelectronics, petroleum

Exports
Chemicals, fuels, foodstuffs, machinery and equipment

Imports
Chemicals, clothing, fuels, foodstuffs, machinery and transport equipment

Port and Harbours
Amsterdam, Delfzijl, Dordrecht, Eemshaven, Groningen, Haarlem, IJmuiden, Maastricht, Rotterdam, Terneuzen, Utrecht, Vlissingen

Airports
There are 27 airports in the Netherlands, of which 20 have paved runways. The international airport hub is at Schiphol.

Weights and Measures
The metric system is used in the Netherlands.

Appliances and Utilities
Voltage in the Netherlands is 220–240 V (60 Hz). Many modern appliances can switch from 110 V to 220 V, so it is a good idea to bring a universal adapter.

ACRONYMS

A6, A9	Two major—and extremely congested—commuter routes on the outskirts of Amsterdam.
ABN-AMRO	A major Dutch bank.
ANWB	The Dutch Touring Association (Algemene Nederlandsche Wielrijders Bond), which provides maps, travel advice and roadside repairs.
Groene Hart	The 'Green Heart' is the rural region of the Netherlands surrounded by Utrecht, Amsterdam, Leiden and Rotterdam.

ING	A major Dutch bank.
Jan Modaal	A fictional character who is the 'average Dutchman' beloved by statisticians and politicians. He has a stay-at-home wife and two children, aged 6 and 11.
KLM	Koninklijke Luchtvaart Maatschappij (Royal Airline Company).
NS	Nederlandse Spoorwegen (Netherlands railway company).
Prinsjesdag	'Prince's Day'—always held on the third Tuesday of September, this is when the government presents its annual budget.
Randstad	The Randstad (peripheral city), i.e. the densely populated urban conglomeration which includes the four main Dutch cities: Amsterdam, Rotterdam, The Hague and Utrecht.
TNT Post	The Dutch post office.

SIXTEEN FAMOUS DUTCH MEN AND WOMEN
Queen Beatrix (1938–)

Queen Beatrix ascended the throne in 1980 when her mother, Queen Juliana, abdicated in her favour. She has proven herself a caring and highly professional monarch. Her commitment to a number of social causes, coupled with her somewhat formal but low-key and scandal-free reign, has made her very popular in the Netherlands. The biggest challenge she now faces is to keep the Dutch monarchy modern, efficient and, above all, in tune with the wishes of the Dutch people.

Crown Prince Willem-Alexander (1967–)

First in the line of succession to the Dutch throne, Willem-Alexander bears the title Prince of Orange. His marriage to the lovely Argentine-born Máxima Zorreguieta in 2002 was well received in the Netherlands and abroad. Willem-Alexander represents the royal family at national and international events and is an avid sportsman.

Johan Cruijff (1947–)

Cruijff is a personally modest but professionally superlative former soccer (football) player who has won many honours in his sport. His expression *Ieder nadeel heb z'n voordeel* ('every disadvantage has its advantage') has passed into common usage. This is how the expression is used: It is bad news when you are stuck in a traffic jam; the good news, though, is that you have time to relax.

Theo van Gogh (1957–2004)

This outspoken filmmaker was a strong advocate of freedom of speech and made enemies on all sides of the political spectrum. He was shot and killed in 2004 by a Muslim extremist who considered van Gogh's controversial film (it was entitled *Submission*) about the position of women in Islam to be anti-Muslim. Van Gogh's death sparked a national controversy over Muslim immigrants in the Netherlands.

Queen Juliana (1909–2004)

Juliana ruled from 1948 to 1980. The Dutch public admired her for her modest lifestyle. She sent her children to public schools, shopped at local stores, abolished outdated formalities such as the curtsey, and was especially interested in the problems of developing countries. By her own wish, she abdicated in favour of her eldest daughter, Beatrix, in 1980, but remained active in public life thereafter. The *New York Times* described her as 'an unpretentious woman of good sense and great goodwill'.

Pim Fortuyn (1948 –2002)

A sociologist and a very colourful but controversial political figure, Fortuyn set up his own populist anti-immigration party in 2002. He denounced Islam as 'backward', claimed that Muslim immigrants were intolerant of the Netherlands' secular and liberal society, and called for an end to immigration. He was shot and killed in 2002 by an animal rights activist who opposed Fortuyn's support for fur farming.

MC Escher (1898–1972)

Known for highly detailed realistic prints that produced remarkable optical and conceptual effects, Escher used multiple and conflicting perspectives to depict landscapes and natural forms. These featured mind-bending spaces and unexpected metamorphoses of one object into another. Widely reproduced, his images won not only public acclaim but also attracted the interest of mathematicians and psychologists.

Queen Wilhemina (1880–1962)

Queen of the Netherlands from 1890 to 1948, Wilhelmina's radio broadcasts from London during World War II made her a symbol of Dutch resistance to the German onslaught and earned her great popularity.

Anne Frank (1929–1945)

Anne Frank was a young Jewish girl who kept a diary during the two years she and her family hid in the back annex of a home on Amsterdam's Prinsengracht during the German occupation of the Netherlands during World War II. She died of typhus in the Bergen-Belsen concentration camp near Hannover, Germany. Her diary, published in 1947 as *The Diary of a Young Girl*, has become a classic in the annals of warfare. In it she wrote, "In spite of everything I still believe that people are really good at heart."

Vincent van Gogh (1853–1890)

Van Gogh is the greatest Dutch painter after Rembrandt. Although his 800 oil paintings and 700 drawings strongly influenced contemporary painters, he sold only one work during his lifetime. His international fame continues to grow. When co-author Ria asked a French doctor which van Gogh painting he preferred, he answered with passion, "*j'aime tout… tout, tout, tout*" ('I love all of them—each and every one of them.') Van Gogh's fame rests not only on his artistic output but also on the drama of his life itself, which was marked by poverty, self-mutilation, mental breakdown and, finally, suicide.

Antony van Leeuwenhoek (1632–1723)

The first microscopist to observe bacteria and protozoa, which he called his 'very little animalcules', van Leeuwenhoek helped to lay the foundation for the scientific disciplines of bacteriology and protozoology. He made his own high-quality microscopes, grinding more than 400 lenses, some of which were no bigger than the head of a pin.

Baruch Spinoza (1632–1677)

This Dutch-Jewish philosopher was the leading advocate of 17th century rationalism. Denounced as atheistic during the 18th century, his works have been carefully studied by professional philosophers since then and have been more appreciated.

Michiel de Ruyter (1607–1676)

One of the Netherlands' greatest admirals, de Ruyter defeated bigger Anglo-French fleets and prevented an invasion of his country by sea. He was mortally wounded while fighting the French in the Mediterranean.

Rembrandt van Rijn (1606–1669)

Rembrandt is arguably the best known painter in the entire history of art. His portraits are highlighted by rich but careful brushwork and a dramatic use of *chiaroscuro* (the interplay of light and shadow). They are also profound studies of character; indeed, he achieved his earliest fame as the most sought-after portrait painter of Amsterdam during the 1630s.

William, Prince of Orange (1533–1584)

William I, the first of the hereditary *stadhouders* (leaders) of the Netherlands, led the revolt against Spanish rule and its Catholicism. He was shot and killed in 1584 by a fanatical Catholic. The Dutch national anthem, *Het Wilhemus*, was written in his honour.

Desiderius Erasmus (1466–1536)

The greatest scholar of the northern Renaissance, Erasmus, was a humanist; that is, he rejected supernaturalism, stressing instead the individual's innate dignity and his or her capacity for self-improvement through reason alone. He was the first editor of the New Testament and played an important role in classical and early Christian studies. Erasmus made major contributions to the liberal tradition of European culture and thought.

CULTURE QUIZ

SITUATION 1

This is the first night you have spent in your newly-rented flat in a trendy neighbourhood of Amsterdam, shortly after your arrival in the Netherlands. You have an important meeting the next day and are looking forward to a good night's sleep. The young tenants of the flat above you, however, are hosting a party to celebrate the ethnic diversity of the Netherlands. Each guest must perform a dance of his or her native land, to the rhythm of authentic music pre-recorded on tape. Although you have already knocked on their door and asked the tenants to make less noise, at 3:30 am the party is still going strong. You:

ⓐ Resolve to speak sternly to the tenants the next day, asking them to be more considerate of the other people in the building.

ⓑ Call the police.

ⓒ Try to ignore the racket and get what rest you can.

ⓓ Knock on their door again and ask if you can join the party and do a dance from your own country.

Comments

Answer **C** is correct for a newcomer. If you had lived in the building for some time and had several other problems with the tenants, answer **B** would be better. Calling the police at this early stage, however, would permanently alienate the tenants, who might otherwise turn out to be friendly and helpful. Speaking sternly to them would probably not result in quieter parties. Without the benefit of musical accompaniment, your own native dance would probably not be a great success.

SITUATION 2

You are an international business executive. Your Dutch boss has invited you to come to his house 'at about eight o'clock' on a given evening. This is the first invitation you have received in the Netherlands. You hear from colleagues in the office that both the boss and his wife greatly value their privacy at home. You:

A Are sure this must be an invitation for a cocktail party. (At your last foreign post, dinner was never eaten before 11:30 pm).

B Believe this is an invitation for a formal dinner. (In your home country, dinner is always served just before 8:00 pm.)

C Realise that this is an invitation for dessert after dinner. (Your own spouse often entertains friends this way at home, after 8:00 pm.)

D Decide, at the risk of making a grave social blunder, to telephone the wife of the boss at home to find out just what this invitation means.

Comments

Answer **D** is correct. Since the Dutch usually eat dinner relatively early (around 6:30–7:00 pm), an invitation for 8:00 pm means coffee and biscuits, perhaps followed by drinks and a light snack. If there is any doubt in your mind about what the hostess has planned, you should certainly call her; but be sure not to give her the impression that you expect dinner.

SITUATION 3

While having dinner at a neighbour's house, you notice that his three young children are giggling at you and whispering to each other in Dutch. They seem to find your table manners very funny, especially your habit of eating with your fork held in your right hand, while keeping your left hand, unused, in your lap. You:

Ⓐ Frown severely and wag your finger at the children so they will stop poking fun at you.

Ⓑ Practise holding the fork in your left hand for the remainder of the meal.

Ⓒ Request that the parents discipline their rowdy children.

Ⓓ Continue to hold the fork in your right hand but ask the parents to explain to the children that in your own country it is considered bad manners to eat with the fork in the left hand!

Comments

Answer **Ⓓ** is correct. Let the parents decide whether discipline is necessary. If you have always held a fork in your right hand, shifting it to the other hand in the middle of dinner is going to be awkward at best.

SITUATION 4

You are a foreign businessman. At a cocktail party you see a pretty, vivacious Dutch lady who is the wife of one of your Dutch colleagues. You have met her socially several times before and each time you got along well and had a nice chat. She recognises you as you approach her. You:

Ⓐ Shake hands with her because to do anything else might be misconstrued by the lady herself or by her husband.

Ⓑ Kiss her lightly on each cheek.

Ⓒ Do nothing because you can't decide what to do.

Comments

Answer ❸ is correct. Dutch men greet their women friends, and Dutch women greet each other, by a light kiss on each cheek. A third kiss can be added for close friends.

SITUATION 5

Before moving to the Netherlands, you spent some years in a country where the royal family was famous for its ostentatious standard of living and for its frequent involvement in scandals. As a result, you have very strong views on this subject. At a coffee break at the office, a Dutch colleague asks you what you think of the Dutch monarchy. You:

❶ Tell him you believe monarchies have no place in modern democracies and that not a euro of public funds should be used to support them.

❷ Praise the selfless dedication of the Dutch House of Orange, its importance as a symbol of national unity and its tradition of keeping a low public profile.

❸ Say that you actually know very little about the House of Orange and ask your colleague to enlighten you.

Comments

Answer ❸ is correct. The Dutch are not highly nationalistic but as a guest you should never criticise their country and especially not the Royal Family, which is universally admired and respected. On the other hand, if you really are a fervent anti-monarchist, you should not go out of your way to praise the Dutch monarchy.

SITUATION 6

You are on a rush hour train in Amsterdam, crowded with *allochtonen* (literally 'other-landers', i.e. recent immigrants or their descendants). A Dutch passenger complains loudly to you, in English, that these *allochtonen* make no effort to speak Dutch, that their religious beliefs clash with the Dutch tradition of religious tolerance, and that they treat women badly. She ends her tirade with an anti-immigrant joke, which is in fact very funny because it is so politically incorrect. You:

A Burst out laughing.

B Maintain a dignified silence.

C Tell her that in your own country, many distinguished citizens come from immigrant backgrounds.

D Ask her if there are any programmes in the Netherlands to help *allochtonen* integrate into Dutch society.

Comments

Given the circumstances, answer **D** is the best one. (In a private conversation, answer **A** would be better because it would be more genuine.) Asking politely about integration programmes should not offend the other passengers. It would also be interesting to hear what the lady has to say on this subject; such programmes do, in fact, exist.

DO'S AND DON'TS

DO'S

- Remember that tolerance is one of the virtues most admired by the Dutch. In practice, this has meant letting people do or say whatever they want (within the limits of the law, of course). A public display of intolerance is a great social blunder. If you have intolerant views, it is wisest to keep them to yourself.

- Realise that if you come from a culture which encourages a self-confident, assertive approach, you should put this characteristic behind you while you are in the Netherlands. A becoming modesty about your achievements is what is valued instead. If you affect an air of authority or superiority, prepare to be criticised.

- Remember, however, that the Dutch are not modest about their own culture but practise a muted nationalism. Being convinced that they are living in an ideal welfare society, they find it difficult to entertain the idea that other countries might be even more advanced than the Netherlands in some respects. As a Portuguese writer and long-time resident in Amsterdam once remarked, the reason why the Dutch travel abroad in such numbers (they are the world's greatest travellers) is simply to confirm their belief that everything is, in all respects, better at home.

- Pay very close attention to your luggage and other worldly goods on the train going from Schiphol Airport to Amsterdam's Central Station, and in the station itself. Muggers—young, older, and sometimes even dressed in a three-piece suit—are very active. They work in groups and will do anything (drop money, offer to help with your luggage, etc) to divert your attention away from your belongings. There are only two bits of good news here: usually the muggers are not violent and the police are trying to improve security. In public areas, be aware of the danger of pickpockets. Leave nothing of value in a parked car. In case of emergency, call the police department on the emergency number 112; if it is not an emergency but you still want to talk to the police, call them on 0900-8844.

- Say 'good morning' and 'good evening' in Dutch (*see the* Glossary *on page 190*) when you meet your neighbour on the staircase or in the street.

- Invite your neighbour for a cup of coffee to make his or her acquaintance as soon as you have settled in.

- Park your car on the outskirts of a big city, e.g. Amsterdam, The Hague, Rotterdam or Utrecht. Parking in big cities is limited and expensive. Illegal parking can result in a ticket or your car being towed, both of which are costly. Instead, use the 'park and ride' facilities to continue your journey by metro or tram. There are, however, a number of underground car parks in city centres. You can reserve a space there by calling tel: 0900-202-2002.

- Buy a ticket before using any kind of public transport: a ticket is always cheaper when bought in advance. A strip of tickets (*strippenkaart*) for the tramway, bus or metro—but not for the trains—can be bought from news agents, train stations, post offices and other outlets. You can buy single tickets from the driver or conductor but they will cost more.

- Board the tram at the rear if you know how many tickets (*strippen*) you will need for your journey. Otherwise, board from the front so that you can ask the driver. Just get on in the front and show your ticket to the driver.

- Ask for a 'bonus card' at your supermarket.

- Remember that the Dutch are famous for their bluntness. From their point of view, what foreigners call bluntness is simply honesty and directness. As one Dutch lady told us, "The Dutch will never invite you into their houses—for dinner, to do some little service for you or just to talk to you—when they don't mean it. And they will let you know sooner rather than later when something doesn't please them. This can be painful."

- Before traveling abroad, Americans (and other non-EU visitors as well) are strongly advised to consult with their medical insurance company to learn whether their policy is valid overseas and whether it will cover emergency

Be careful of what you say in public, especially criticisms of the Royal Family, Dutch policies, minorities, etc.

expenses, especially medical repatriation, which can be ruinously expensive.

- Do take a ticket. Many small stores have ticket machines to avoid disputes over whose turn it is to be served. There are also ticket machines in post offices.

DON'TS

- Don't extend to the Dutch what might be called a 'California invitation'; that is, inviting someone to your home merely as an expression of goodwill or as a polite gesture. The Dutch will not understand that such an invitation ('You simply must come see us!') is not to be taken seriously.
- Do not criticise, especially in public, any Dutch policies on subjects where negative statements might conceivably offend your listeners. Until you know people well, it is best to avoid criticising the Royal Family, ethnic minorities, alternative lifestyles, drugs, crime, etc.
- Don't flatter your Dutch friends or associates by paying them too many polite compliments. They will not believe

you and will think you are exaggerating. Keep as close to the truth as possible.

- Don't walk along the lanes reserved for bicycles—it drives locals mad! There are express bike lanes through Dutch cities. These are usually clearly marked with a bike symbol.
- Tipping of waiters, taxi drivers, etc, is not required in the Netherlands. If you want to show your appreciation for especially good service, a tip should not be more than 10 per cent of the total amount due.
- Do not ride a bicycle in pedestrian areas: get off and push it.
- While the Netherlands allows possession of a tiny amount of soft drugs, these must not be consumed in public places but only in the 'coffee shops' or in private residences. Possession and use of hard drugs—and of weapons—is, however, strictly forbidden.
- It is unwise to change money in the centre of big cities where muggers await the unwary, or visit the red light district or down-at-heel sections of a big city after dark. The latter are a mugger's delight and are also frequented by junkies.
- It is rude to start eating immediately after dinner is served. Wait until your hostess starts.
- Don't forget a birthday. This is a major social blunder.

GLOSSARY

The first entry is the word or phrase in English; the second is the word or phrase in Dutch; and the third is an approximate pronunciation in English of the Dutch word. Note that the Dutch guttural *g* or *gh* has no counterpart in English and cannot be recorded accurately without recourse to phonetic spelling. 'Kh' is used here to approximate this guttural. Choose one of the transliterated words below with 'kh' in it and ask a Dutch speaker to pronounce it.

English	Dutch	Pronunciation
Mr	*Mijnheer*	menayr
Mrs	*Mevrouw*	mevrow
Yes	*Ja*	yah
No	*Nee*	ney
Thank you	*Dank U*	dank u
You're welcome	*Geen dank* or *niets te danken*	kheyn dank / neets te danken
Please	*Alstublieft*	ahstoobleeft
Excuse me	*Neemt u mij niet kwalijk* or *Excuseert u mij*	neymt u mey neet kwalik / excuseert u mey
Goodbye (familiar)	*Dag*	dakh
Goodbye (formal)	*Dag mijnheer X* or *Dag mevrouw XX*	
See you	*Tot ziens*	tot zeens
Good morning	*Goedemorgen*	khoodemorkhe
Good afternoon	*Goedemiddag*	khoodemidakh
Good evening	*Goedenavond*	khoodenavond
Good night	*Slaap lekker*	slaap lekker
I don't understand	*Ik begrijp u niet*	Ik begryp u neet

English	Dutch	Pronunciation
Do you speak…?	*Spreekt u …?*	Spreakt u…"
English	*Engels*	Engels
French	*Frans*	Frans
German	*Duits*	Douts
Spanish	*Spaans*	Spaans
Exit	*Uitgang*	outkhang
Entrance	*Ingang*	innkhang
Pull	*Trekken*	trekken
Push	*Duwen*	duwen
Open	*Open*	open
Closed	*Gesloten*	khesloten
To all trains	*Naar de treinen*	naar de treynen
Tickets	*Plaatsbewijzen*	plaatsbeveyzen
Where is…	*Waar is…*	waar is…
Domestic travel (within the Netherlands)	*Binnenland*	binnenland
International travel	*Buitenland*	bouteland
Taxi, please	*Taxi, alstublieft*	taxi, ahstoobleeft
How much is it?	*Hoeveel kost het?*	hooveyl kost het?
One-way ticket	*Enkele reis*	enkele reys
Return-trip ticket	*Retour*	retour
One ticket to… please	*Een kaartje naar… alstublieft*	un kaartjenaar… ahstoobleeft
Left	*Links*	links
Right	*Rechts*	rekhts
Straight ahead	*Rechtdoor*	rekhtdoor
Up	*Omhoog*	omhaukh
Down	*Omlaag* or *naar beneden*	omlaakh / naar benayden
Map	*Plattegrond*	plattekhrond

English	Dutch	Pronunciation
Train	*Trein*	treyn
Bus	*Bus*	bus
Subway or Underground	*Metro*	maytro
Airport	*Vliegveld*	vliekhfelt
Train station	*Station*	stashon
Bus station	*Busstation*	bus stashon
Departure	*Vertrek*	furtrek
Arrival	*Aankomst*	ahnkomst
Customs	*Douane*	doo-ahne
Car rental	*Aautoverhuur*	autoverhuur
Room	*Kamer*	kahmer
Reservation	*Reservering*	reserveering
Are there any vacancies for tonight?	*Is er nog een kamer vrij?*	Is er nokh een kahmer vry?
No vacancies	*Vol*	Vol
How much does this cost?	*Wat kost dit?*	Wat kost dit?
What is this?	*Wat is dit?*	Wat iz dit?
I'll buy it	*Ik koop het* or *ik neem deze*	ik kope het / ik naym dayze
Do you have...?	*Heeft u...?*	hayft u ...?
Passport	*Paspoort*	paspoort
Driver's licence	*Rijbewijs*	rybewys
Stamps	*Postzegels*	postzeykhels
Post office	*Postkantoor*	postkantore
Bank	*Bank*	bank
Police station	*Politiebureau*	poleetzeeburoh
Hospital	*Ziekenhuis*	zeekenhouse
Pharmacy or chemist	*Apotheek*	apotake

English	Dutch	Pronunciation
Store, shop	*Winkel*	vinkel
Museum	*Museum*	muzeyum
Restaurant	*Restaurant*	restowran
School	*School*	skhole
Church	*Kerk*	cairk
I	*Ik*	ik
We	*wij*	wey
You (informal)	*Jij*	yey
You (informal plural)	*Jullie*	yallee
You (formal, singular and plural)	*U*	u
He	*Hij*	hi
She	*Zij*	zay
It	*Het*	het
They	*Zij*	zay
Wife	*Vrouw* or *echtgenote*	vrow / ekhtkhenowte
Husband	*Man* or *echtgenoot*	man / ekhtkhenoat
Daughter	*Dochter*	dokhter
Son	*Zoon*	zone
Mother	*Moeder*	mooder
Father	*Vader*	vahder
Friend	*Vriend*	vreend
What is your name?	*Hoe heet je?* or *Hoe heet u?*	hoo heyt yey / hoo heyt u?
How are you?	*Hoe gaat het?*	hoo khat het?
Good	*Goed*	khoot
Bad	*Slecht*	slekht

English	Dutch	Pronunciation
Toilets, restrooms	*Toiletten* or *WC*	twaletten / vey say
Where is the restroom?	*Waar zijn de toiletten?*	wair zeyn de twaletten?
Men's toilet	*Herentoilet*	heerentwalet
Ladies' toilet	*Damestoilet*	damestwalet
Street	*Straat*	straat
Bridge	*Brug*	brukh
Lake	*Meer*	meer
Sea	*Zee*	zey
River	*Rivier*	reeveer
Day	*Dag*	dakh
Today	*Vandaag*	vandaag
Tomorrow	*Morgen*	morkhen
Yesterday	*Gisteren*	khisteren
Monday	*Maandag*	maandakh
Tuesday	*Dinsdag*	dinsdakh
Wednesday	*Woensdag*	woonsdakh
Thursday	*Donderdag*	donderdakh
Friday	*Vrijdag*	vreydakh
Saturday	*Zaterdag*	zahterdakh
Sunday	*Zondag*	zondakh
Breakfast	*Ontbijt*	ontbeyt
Lunch	*Lunch*	lunch
Dinner	*Diner*	dinay
Vegetarian	*Vegetarier*	veykhetareer
Meat	*Vlees*	vlays
Beef	*Rundvlees*	rundvleys
Pork	*Varkensvlees*	varkensvleys
Fish	*Vis*	vis
Chicken	*Kip*	kip

English	Dutch	Pronunciation
Vegetables	*Groente*	khroonte
Potato	*Aardappel*	aardappel
Rice	*Rijst*	reyst
Dessert	*Nagerecht*	nakherekht
Can I have my bill, please	*De rekening, alstublieft*	de reykening, ahstoobleeft
Zero	*Nul*	nul
One	*Een*	eyn
Two	*Twee*	twey
Three	*Drie*	dree
Four	*Vier*	veer
Five	*Vijf*	veyf
Six	*Zes*	zes
Seven	*Zeven*	zayven
Eight	*Acht*	akht
Nine	*Negen*	neykhen
Ten	*Tien*	teen
Congratulations!	*Gefeliciteerd!*	khefayleeceeteerd

RESOURCE GUIDE

EMERGENCIES & HEALTH
Emergency Numbers
Police, ambulance, or fire brigade   **112**
Police (non-emergency)   **0900-8844**
Road service (for car breakdowns)   **088-269-2888**

Hospitals
For medical emergencies, go to the nearest hospital, which will be listed in the *Yellow Pages* under *Ziekenhuizen*. Some of the best hospitals are:

- Academic Medical Centre Amsterdam
  Meibergdreef 9, 1105 AZ Amsterdam
  Tel: (020) 566-9111
- Academic Hospital Vrije Universiteit Amsterdam
  De Boelelaan 1117, 1081 HV Amsterdam
  Tel: (020) 444-4444
- Academic Hospital Nijmegen St Radboud
  G. Grooteplein Z10, 6525 GA Nijmegen
  Tel: (024) 361-1111
- Academic Hospital Rotterdam Dijkzigt
  Dr Molewaterplein 40, 3015 GD Rotterdam
  Tel: (010) 463-9222
- Het Oogziekenhuis, Rotterdam
  (specialises in eye diseases)
  Schiedamse Vest 180, 3011 BH Rotterdam
  Tel: (010) 401-7777
- Academic Hospital Utrecht
  (with a special Heart and Lung Institute),
  Heidelberglaan 100, 3584 CX Utrecht
  Tel: (030) 250-9111
- Diaconessenziekenhuis, Utrecht
  Bosboomstraat 1, 3582 KE Utrecht
  Tel: (030) 256-6566
- Academic Hospital Leiden
  Albinusdreef 2, 2333 ZA Leiden
  Tel: (071) 526-9111

Dental Clinics

Finding a dentist can be a problem in the Netherlands as most dentists have a waiting list. There are Internet sites where you can find a dentist near you but they are all in Dutch. For dental emergencies, look in the *Yellow Pages* under *Tandartsen*. For non-emergency dental treatment, it is probably best to ask a Dutch friend or neighbour for advice.

Medical Services and Contacts

For birth control or abortion, see your doctor or go to the nearest hospital or contact STISAN, an umbrella organisation of abortion clinics. Visit its website:

http://www.stisan.nl

or contact it in person at Sarphatistraat 620-626, 1018 AV Amsterdam, tel: (020) 624-5426.

Lost and Found

If you lose something while on a train, it should eventually end up in Utrecht at:

Centraal Bureau Gevonden Voorwerpen

2e Daalsedijk 4, 3551 EJ Utrecht

Tel: (0900) 321-2100

It will be kept there for three months, after which time it will be sold. For objects lost on other means of transportation, check with the company concerned. It will have a lost and found department.

Facilities for the Handicapped

At Schiphol Airport, there is a free service from
- International Help for the Disabled (IHD)
  Tel: (020) 316-1417

When assistance from the point of entry (e.g. taxi stop, bus stop, car, train station) to the airport is required, passengers can contact Intergom Airport Caddy, which provides this service on behalf of Schiphol Airport. Tel: (020)405-7900; e-mail: assistentie@airportcaddy.nl.

Disabled people who need assistance for travel by train can call the
- Bureau Assistentieverlening Gehandicapten
  Tel: (030) 235 7822
  People with a speech disability can fax: (030) 235-3935.
  Note that to use these assistance services, you should call before 2:00 pm one working day before the travel is to take place.

HOME & FAMILY
Accommodation Information
The property market in the Netherlands has soared over the last decade. Prices have tripled and it is difficult to get what you want. Make sure that your real estate agent (*makelaar*) is a member of the Netherlands Association for Real Estate Agents (NVM). Its Internet site is

http://www.funda.nl.

The *Yellow Pages* carry a NVM advertisement listing its members; look under *Makelaars en adviseurs onroerende goederen*. Members have agreed to abide by NVM rules designed to protect the client.

A sample of real estate agents includes:
- Meeus, Laan van Nieuw Oost Indie 123-125,
  Postbus 93424, 2509 AK The Hague
  Tel: (070) 358-2800, fax: (070) 358-2915
- Frisia Makelaars
  Javastraat 1a, 2585 AA The Hague
  Tel: (070) 342-0101, fax: (070) 364- 4232
  Website: http://www.frisia.nl
- Peter Rottgerink Makelaars
  Breitnerlaan 287, The Hague
  Tel: (070) 324-5566
- Jacobus Recourt Makelaars
  Nieuwezijds Voorburgwal 298, 1012 RT Amsterdam
  Tel: (020) 675-0606
- NVM van Staveren Makelaardij og
  De Lairessestraat 40, 1071 PB Amsterdam
  Tel: (020) 675-0626

- Beekman Makelaardij NVM
  Maasstraat 79, 1078 HE Amsterdam
  Tel: (020) 679-2020
- Makelaars Stad en Land NVM
  Vredehofweg 70, 3062 ES Rotterdam
  Tel: (010) 452-6666;
- NVM Makelaars Waltmann & Co
  Maliesingel 18, 3581 BE Utrecht
  Tel: (030) 231-3035.

Childcare and Schools

For childcare, check with your Town Hall for local addresses.

- General information about childcare can be obtained from:
  SKON (Stichting Kinderopvang Nederland)
  Energieweg 1, 3542 DZ Utrecht
  Tel: (0346) 559-500
  http://www.skon.nl

- If you want to check up on a childcare centre, you can get in touch with
  BOINK (an organisation of parents)
  Tel: (030) 231-7914, daily between 9:00 am–1:00 pm
  http://www.boink.info.

- International schools can be found on the website of the Foundation for International Education in the Netherlands (SIO).
  http://www.sio/nl/regionmap.html

- To help you put a child into a Dutch school, the educational system is explained on the website:
  http://www.studyin.nl

- Other information about education can be obtained from the Dutch government's centre for public service information, known as:
  Postbus 51
  Tel: 0800-8051
  Website: http://www.postbus51.nl

To order leaflets and other publications in English or other languages, click 'Brochures' at the top of Postbus 51 website. If you are looking for Dutch government websites in English, use the external link on the right.

Domestic Help
Try checking with your Town Hall. Ask your Dutch friends. They may be able to find domestic help.

Budget Hotels
The Netherlands offers a wide range of guesthouses and hotels for budget travellers. For information, contact the nearest VVV office—this is a truly excellent tourist information service—at http:// www.vvv.nl. There you will be able to find the local telephone number you need.

MANAGING YOUR MONEY
Taxes
Tax reforms in 2001 brought about a number of changes for employees recruited from outside the Netherlands, or assigned from the Netherlands, by a withholding agent. You can learn about them from two Internet sites:
- http://www.minfin.nl
- http://www.belastingdienst.nl

or by calling the Tax Information Line, tel: 0800-0543. This number is not available from a mobile phone.

Insurance
If you are not insured when you arrive in the Netherlands, you can get a 'OOM-insurance' (Global Visitor insurance) covering health and travel by contacting the nearest office of the ANWB or by calling tel: 0800-0503 or via website http://www.oomverzekeringen.nl.

The ANWB is the Netherlands' largest tourism, recreation and automobile travel organisation. In many countries, the local Netherlands Embassy will not issue a visa without proof of such insurance.

Cash

As it is in many European countries, the euro is now the official currency of the Netherlands. Coins and bills are available in the standard range of denominations.

Whatever bank you choose, make sure that it gives you a card you can use internationally. The Netherlands is a small country: it is likely that you will travel to a neighbouring country as well. Most cards can be used internationally but it does not hurt to double check. Look for the Maestro and Cirrus logos since these networks allow you to withdraw money in most countries.

ATMs are called *geldautomaten* or *pinautomaten* in Dutch. Every reasonable sized town in the Netherlands has some of them; bigger cities have many. You can use any bank's card in almost all other banks' ATMs in the Netherlands, but check with your bank about possible charges for doing so. Thus if you have an ABN-AMRO card, you can also use it at the ING *pinautomaat* at no extra charge. This service is known as *gastgebruik* (guest use). You can use it only once every 24 hours.

Banking

Well-known banks include:

- ABN-AMRO Holding NV
  PO Box 600, 1000 AP Amsterdam
  In the Netherlands, call 0900 00 24 for information (choose option 4 for an English-language menu). From outside the Netherlands, call (+ 31-10) 241-1720
  Website: http://www.abnamro.com
- Rabobank Nederland
  P.O. Box 17100, 3500 HG Utrecht
  Tel: (030) 0900-0907, fax: (030) 216-2672
  Wesbite:http://www.rabobank.nl
- ING Groep NV
  Amstelveenseweg 500, 1081 KL Amsterdam.
  Tel: (020) 541-5411, fax: (020) 541-5497
  WebsiteL http://www.inggroup.com

Borrowing Money

If you need to borrow money to buy a property, first go to one of the approximately 185 *hypotheekshops* in the Netherlands. There you will get objective advice, free of charge, on what you can afford. It is often cheaper to get a mortgage from a *hypotheekshop* than from a bank. For loans for other purposes, go to a major bank.

ENTERTAINMENT & LEISURE
Restaurants

There are so many restaurants in the Netherlands (more than 1,000 in Amsterdam alone) that trying to single out the best ones is unfair to the rest. Moreover, restaurants wax and wane, so a place that merited, say, two stars at one point may lose them under new and less professional management. At the upper end of the scale, however, experienced diners with good taste and deep pockets—"the happy few," one Dutch friend calls them—will appreciate:

- De Librije
  Broerenkerkplein 13, Zwolle
  Tel: (038) 421-2083
  Website: http://www.delibrije.nl
  This fine restaurant is located in a medieval monastery in the lovely town of Zwolle.

Cafés

These come in many styles:
- student cafés
- café/diners
- 'brown cafés', so called because their walls and ceilings have been browned by, in some cases, literally hundreds of years of tobacco smoke
- 'grand cafés', which offer not only drinks but also snacks and a reading table with Dutch and international newspapers and magazines

One of the most famous brown cafés in Amsterdam is the Café Hoppe, Spui 18-20, tel: (020) 420-4420, founded in 1670.

Please remember that, as noted in the section on drugs, 'coffee shops' in the Netherlands sell small amounts of soft drugs, not coffee.

Shopping Districts and Size Conversions

The Netherlands' most popular department store is HEMA (Hollandse Eenheidsprijzen Maatschappij). Nearly every town will have a HEMA store. No store is more truly Dutch: everyone goes there and its sausage is famous. Major department stores include:

- De Bijenkorf and V&D (Vroom en Dreesman), which are located in many cities.
- De Bonneterie, an upmarket store, is located in Amsterdam, The Hague, Laren and Heemstede.

There are IKEA shops in 12 locations in the Netherlands.

Good markets include Albert Cuypmarket, located in the De Pijp quarter. Another good market is Rotterdam's Centremarket, which is located on the Binnenrotteterrein. With about 500 merchants, a very wide range of items —flowers, fish, books, etc—is offered for sale. Utrecht offers Hoog-Catharijne, a mall which is located in the same complex as the train station.

Here are size conversions (*Benelux* is an abbreviation for Belgium/Netherlands/Luxembourg). To double-check sizes when you are buying shoes via the Internet, use the handy online conversion website: http://www.onlineconversion.com. This site has calculated nearly every possible size conversion.

Men's suits

British	34	36	38	40	42	44	46	48	
Benelux	44	46	48	50	52	54	56	58/60	62
American	34	36	38	40	42	44	46	48	

Men's shirts

British	14	14½	15	15½	16	16½	17
Benelux	36	37	38	39	40	41	42
American	14	14½	15	15½	16	16½	17

Men's shoes

British	6½	7½	8½	9½	10½	11½
Benelux	40½	41½	42½	43½	44½	45½
American	7	8	9	10	11	12

Women's dresses

British	8	10	12	14	16	18
Benelux	34	36	38	40	42	44
American	6	8	10	12	14	16

Women's shoes

British	4	4½	5½	6½	7½	8½
Benelux	36½	37	38	39	40	41
American	6	6½	7½	8½	9½	10½

Nightspots

Other big Dutch cities have a good range of nightspots too, but Amsterdam is definitely one of the entertainment capitals of the world. It offers nightlife in abundance—bars with live music, casinos, discos, theatres and X-rated entertainment in the red light district. There is literally something for every taste. In Amsterdam, most of the cafés, restaurants, nightclubs and discos are located around the Leidseplein and the Rembrandtplein areas. Visit the website http://www.amsterdamtourist.com for useful information on the nightspots and the many other attractions this lovely city offers.

Cinemas

Films in the Netherlands are shown in their original language, with subtitles in Dutch. For listings for what is on in all major Dutch towns, look for the *Filmladders* in the Wednesday paper, call tel: 0900-9363, or check the Internet site:

http://www.filmladder.nl

(enter the town of your choice under *kies je stad* and all the cinemas will pop up).

Theatres

Theatre performances are usually in Dutch; only a few are in English. For information on theatres and concerts (and for bookings), you can also call the Reserveerlijn (a national ticket reservation line), tel: 0900-300-5000.

Bookshops

The easiest way to find bookshops in the Netherlands is to visit the website:

http://www.boekenwinkels.startkabel.nl

Amsterdam

Good bookshops in Amsterdam include:

- Atheneaum
  Spui 14-16
  Tel: (020) 622-6248
  Website: http:// www.athenaeum.nl
- Scheltema Holkema Vermeulen
  Koningsplein 20
  Tel: (020) 523-1411
- The English Bookshop
  Lauriergracht 71hs
  Tel: (020) 626-4230
- Waterstone's Bookshop
  Kalverstraat 152
  Tel: (020) 638-3821
- Kookboekhandel.com
  Haarlemmerdijk 133
  1013 KG Amsterdam
  Tel: (020) 622 4768
  This is the only cookbook shop in the Benelux with cookbooks from all over the world in every language. Any cookbook can be ordered.
- The American Book Centre
  Kalverstraat 185
  Tel: (020) 625-5537
  Website: www.abc.nl

Rotterdam

The largest bookstore in the Netherlands is in Rotterdam:

- Donner Boekhandel
  Lijnbaan 150
  Tel: (010) 413-2070

The Hague

The Hague has:

- Paagman
  Frederik Hendriklaan 217
  Tel: (070) 338-3838
- Verwijs
  de Passage 39
  Tel: (070) 311-4848l
- The American Book Centre
  Lange Poten 23
  Tel: (070) 364-2742
  Website: http://www.abc.nl

Utrecht

Utrecht offers:

- Broese Wristers
  Stadhuisbrug 5
  Tel: (030) 233-5200

Leiden

- Kooyker
  Breestraat 93
  Tel: (071) 516-0500

Libraries

Visit the website:

http://www.bibliotheek.startpagina.nl

All public libraries are listed on this site. In addition to such specialised libraries as Amsterdam's Gastronomic Library [2e Oosterparkstraat 261, tel: (020) 694-3403], visits by appointment only. There is a wide range of other libraries. Here are a few of them.

Amsterdam
Openbare Bibliotheek Amsterdam
Oosterdokskade 143
Tel: (020) 523-0900

Rotterdam
Centrale Bibliotheek
Hoogstraat 110
Tel: (010) 281-6100

The Hague
Openbare Bibliotheek
Spui 68
Tel: (070) 353-4455
Website: http://www.bibliotheekdenhaag.nl (This website is
in English.)

Utrecht
Openbare Bibliotheek
Oude Gracht 167
Tel: (030) 286-1800

Cultural and Social Organisations
See the following section on Clubs. Have a look, too, at
http://www.dutchnews.nl. It includes an extensive What's On
section (updated every Thursday), classified advertisements,
columnists, comments and useful links for expatriates.

Clubs
There are over 400 Rotary clubs in the Netherlands. For
details, check the website: http://www.rotary.nl
Here are some international clubs.

The Hague
- Societeit Nieuwe of Litteraire de Witte
  Plein 24
  Tel: (070) 360-7933
  http://www.societeitdewitte.nl
  (Probably the most elite club, attracting diplomats, etc.)

- The American Women's Club
  Nieuwe Duinweg 25
  Tel: (070) 350-6007
  http://www.awcthehague.org
- The British Women's Club
  Plein 24
  Tel: (070) 346-1973
  http://bwclubthehague.demon.nl
- International Women's Contact
  Vierloper 10
  Tel: (070) 355-8863
  http://www.iwcthehague.nl

Amsterdam

- The American Women's Club
  Noordbrabantstraat 152 bg
  Tel: (020) 644-3531
- The British Society of Amsterdam
  Tel: (06) 5170-8081
  http://www.britishsocietyofamsterdam.org

Physical Fitness Centres & Sports Facilities

Sport is an important part of life in the Netherlands. It is a good idea to join a sports club. There are more than 30,000 sports clubs with a total of nearly five million members. Every big hotel has a fitness club. A welcome new development is that some therapists now offer sports training (under supervision) as part of their practice. An excellent pastime is to bicycle near or to walk along the extensive beaches and sand dunes of the Netherlands. This is a fine activity for individuals, couples and families alike. It takes place in a quiet, non-polluted environment which can, with proper clothing, be enjoyed all year round. Skating is a popular winter sport. The Netherlands offers many frozen lakes and dozens of ice rinks. The most famous skating event is Friesland's 136-mile-long *Elfstedentocht* ('eleven-town tour').

A unique and famous event in the Netherlands is known as the Four-Days Marches (Vierdaagse). These seem to be the largest scheduled civilian walking event in the world. Each year, tens of thousands of people take part, coming from all over the world to hike through Nijmegen's beautiful countryside. In addition, the Four Days Marches Festival takes place during the same week. These two events draw a total of more than one million visitors.

Museums
Nearly all the museums in the Netherlands are described on the Internet site http://www.museum.nl. As mentioned earlier, the museumcard is very useful.

Amsterdam
Amsterdam itself is said to have 'more museums per square inch' than any other city in the world. These include:
- Van Gogh Museum
  Paulus Potterstraat
  Tel: (020) 570-5200
  (Contains 200 paintings and 500 drawings by Van Gogh.)
- Rembrandthuis
  Jodenbreestraat
  Tel: (020) 520-0400
  (Where Rembrandt lived for 20 years.)
- Rijksmuseum
  Stadhouderskade 42
  Tel: (020) 673-2121
  (By far the largest museum in the Netherlands.)
- Stedelijk Museum of Modern Art
  Paulus Potterstraat 13
  Tel: (020) 573-2911
  (It houses one of the major collections of modern art in the Netherlands.)

The Hague
The Hague has:
- The Gemeentemuseum
  Stadhouderslaan 41
  Tel: (070) 338-1111
  (Extensively renovated in 1998.)

- The Mauritshuis
  Korte Vijverberg 8
  Tel: (070) 302-3456
  (Housed in one of the Netherlands' most outstanding classic buildings and celebrated for its collection of Dutch masterpieces from the 17th century.)
- Escher in het Paleis (Escher in the Palace)
  Lange Voorhout 74
  2514 EH 's-Gravenhage
  Tel: (070) 427-7730
  Dedicated to the work of the Netherlands' most famous graphic artist, M C Escher (1898–1972). Nearly all his prints are exhibited here.
- The Museon
  Stadhouderslaan 41
  Tel: (070) 338-1338
  (The greatest and most popular scientific museum in the country.)

Rotterdam

- Museum Boijmans Van Beuningen
  Museumpark 18–20
  Tel: (010) 441-9400
  (A multi-faceted museum covering the period from the Middle Ages to the present day.)

Utrecht

Utrecht has the recently-renovated Centraal Museum [Nicolaaskerkhof 10, tel: (030) 236-2362], which has the largest collection in the world on the Dutch designer, architect and cabinet maker Gerrit Rietveld (1888–1964) and also has very good collections of contemporary art and 17th century Utrecht masters. It also has a helpful information centre where you can arrange to see works of art which are not currently exhibited.

Haarlem

Haarlem has the Frans Hals Museum [Groot Heiligland 62, tel: (023) 511-5775], one of the better places to view the old masters.

Music

For classical music, start with Amsterdam. Its Concertgebouw [Concertgebouwplein 2-6, tel: (020) 671-8345] reportedly has the best acoustics of any concert hall in the world. The resident Royal Concertgebouw Orchestra is among the world's best. The Muziektheater has about 1,600 seats and is one of the largest theatres in Amsterdam. Two companies are based there: the Nederlandse Opera and the Nationale Ballet.

Alternative Lifestyle

There is little, if any, social discrimination in the Netherlands against gays or lesbians. Same-sex couples can marry. In the workplace, sexual discrimination or harassment is illegal and can be punished by stiff fines. Alternative lifestyles can therefore be practised openly, provided that the people involved behave 'normally' (*gewoon*), which is a great virtue in the eyes of the Dutch.

There is a Gay & Lesbian Switchboard [tel: (020) 623-6565; website: http://www.switchboard.nl] that serves as an information, support and referral service for gay men and lesbians. The general policy of the Dutch seems to be: everything is permitted, as long as you don't try to impose it on other citizens and thereby violate their own rights.

TRANSPORT & COMMUNICATIONS
City and Country Codes for Telephone Numbers

Country code   31

Selected city codes

Amsterdam	020
The Hague	070
Rotterdam	010
Utrecht	030

Telephone Service Numbers

Directory assistance

domestic numbers	**1888**
international numbers	**0900-8418**
Customer Services (telephone and Internet)	**0900-0244**

Other useful numbers are:

Operator	0800-0410
Collect calls	0800-0101
KPN Internet	0900-1905

Post Office

You can find a post office by looking for a red rectangular sign marked *Postkantoor*. These offices are often located in a Bruna bookstore. For Post Customer Service, call tel: (058) 233-3333.

Bus, Train, and Taxi Information
Trains and Buses

For information on how to get from one place to another, call tel: 0900-9292 (domestic travel) or tel: 0900-9296 (international travel). See also Internet sites:

- http://www.9292ov.nl
- http://www.ns.nl (available in English as well)
- http://www.nstravel.nl

Taxis

- Schiphol Travel Taxi
  Tel: 0900-8876 (from within the Netherlands)
  Tel. (+31) 339-4768 (from abroad)
  You can also book via the website http://www.schiphol.nl
- Amsterdam, tel: (020) 777-7777
- The Hague, tel: (070) 383-0830
- Rotterdam, tel: (010) 462-6060
- Utrecht, tel: (030) 230-0400

MEDIA
Newspapers and Magazines

The latest news from the Netherlands, in English, is on the Internet newspaper site http://www.dutchnews.nl. You can subscribe to a free daily Internet newsletter. This site also has an Expat Directory, which is very useful.

All major foreign newspapers are available in the Netherlands. *De Telegraaf* is the Netherlands' most popular newspaper. *NRC-Handelsblad* (liberal orientation), *Trouw* (Christian orientation) and *Het Financieele Dagblad* (economic orientation) are perhaps the best independent newspapers. *Het Financieele Dagblad* also has an English section. Foreign newspapers and magazines are usually available at major train stations.

There are also four free newspapers in Dutch: *Metro*, *Spits*, *De Pers* and *Dag*. They are very popular and are available in railway stations, supermarkets and bookshops.

Television and Radio

Cable, former telephone and Internet companies provide good radio, television, internet and telephone service. It is best to subscribe to this entire package with one company. Many houses in the Netherlands already have a built-in outlet. Most cable companies provide international channels, e.g. CNN, BBC, Belgian, French, Italian and German channels for both television and radio.

LANGUAGE
Language Institutes and Classes

The chances are very good that every Dutch person you meet will be able to speak at least some English. Nevertheless, learning Dutch is still a good idea. Every Dutch university offers a language course. There are many other language courses offered as well. One good place is:

- Berlitz Language Centre
  Brouwersweg 100, 6216 EG Maastricht
  Tel: (043) 346-7231
  http://www.berlitz.nl
  (Berlitz also has centres in other Dutch cities)

RELIGION & SOCIAL WORK
Religious Institutions

The easiest way to find a religious institution of your choice is to ask at the local Town Hall.

Volunteer Organisations
Amsterdam

- Union of Volunteers
  Brouwersgracht 270B
  Tel: (020) 620-7068
- The Volunteercentre
  Hartenstraat 16
  Tel: (020) 530-1220

The Hague

- Union of Volunteers
  Korte Poten 9A
  Tel: (070) 365-7885

Rotterdam

- Help service Volunteers Info/advice
  Westersingel 23
  Tel: (010) 436-3090
- Union of Volunteers
  Oostzeedijk 60
  Tel: (010) 413-0877

Utrecht

- Netherlands Organisation Volunteerwork
  Plompetorengracht 17
  Tel: (030) 750-9095
- SIW International Volunteers
  Willenstraat 7
  Tel: (030) 231-7721

GENERAL COUNTRY INFORMATION
Necessary Documents

Documentary requirements for the Netherlands (passports, visas and perhaps driving licences) depend on which country you are from. Check with the nearest Dutch embassy or consulate well before your departure date.

Pre-entry Vaccinations
In general, these are not required but if you have any doubts, check with the nearest Dutch embassy or consulate. If you are arriving by air, your airline will be able to tell you.

Embassies
There are more than 90 embassies in The Hague. You can get their addresses, telephone numbers, etc. from the Internet site of the Netherlands Ministry of Foreign Affairs at:

http://www.minbuza.nl

This site is in Dutch but can be used by English-speakers. To use it, first click *'ambassades en consulaten'*, then *'buitenlandse vertegenwoordigingen in Nederland'*, then *'Adressen Buitenlandse vertegenwoordigingen'*, and then click on the English flag.

Another Dutch Internet site with the same information is:

http://www.detelefoongids.nl

Go to *'Bedrijven'*, fill in (under *'Rubriek'*) *'Ambassades en Consulaten'*, and in box number two, *'Woonplaats'* Den Haag.

Internet Search Engines
A Dutch Internet site for search engines lists the following:
- Altavista (English)
- Yahoo (English)
- Ilse
- Google
- MSN
- Vindex

General and Tourist Advice on the Internet
The Dutch tourist office VVV and the travel organisation ANWB, both mentioned above, are especially useful. Have a look too, at the following websites:
- http://www.visitholland.nl
- http://www.minbuza.nl
- http://www.overheid.nl (click on 'English')

Other useful websites are:

- http://www.expatica.com
  An English-language news and information source for expatriates in the Netherlands. The news pages are updated daily.
- http://www.access-nl.org
  This is the English-language website of ACCESS, a non-profit organisation that helps English-speaking expatriates and their families adjust to the Netherlands. The site also provides useful information on travelling in the Netherlands.
- http://www. elynx.nl
  Focuses on the English-speaking community in the Netherlands. Elynx organises many social activities.
- http//www.radionetherlands.nl
  Extensive news and views from a Dutch perspective, plus a web page for every feature programme.
- http://www.xpat.nl
  Offers a variety of publications with essential information for all aspects of expatriate life in the Netherlands, including addresses of sales outlets, from which you can order online.

Immigration, Residency and Nationality

Since these matters are subject to change, check with your nearest Dutch embassy or consulate well before your planned departure date.

See also the Internet sites http://www.ind.nl and http://www.naarnederland.nl. Both are available in Dutch and in English.

BUSINESS INFORMATION
Business Organisations

Chambers of Commerce offer a wide range of services for entrepreneurs. Amsterdam's Chamber of Commerce is:

- Kamer van Koophandel
  De Ruyterkade 5
  1013 AA Amsterdam
  Tel: (020) 531-4000

Website: http://www.amsterdam.kvk.nl
It can give you details on the other Chambers of Commerce, which are located in Lelystad, Leeuwarden, Apeldoorn and Utrecht.

Real Estate

To find a place to buy in the location you want to live in, try visiting: http://www.funda.nl.

This reliable site is in Dutch only but it is very useful. All you have to do is to fill in the location where you want to live and the amount you want to spend.

You may also want to get in touch with:

- Nederlandse Vereniging voor Makelaars (NVM)
  Postbus 2222
  3430 DC Nieuwegein
  Tel: (030) 608-5185
  Website: http://www.nvm.nl

Automobiles

- Bovag (Bond van Garagehouders: a union of garage owners or car dealers)
  Postbus 1100
  3980 DC Bunnik
  Tel: (030) 659-5211

Travel by automobile:

- ANWB
  Wassenaarseweg 220
  2596 EC Den Haag
  Tel: (070) 314-7147
  ANWB Contact Centre tel: (088)269-2222;
  Car assistance tel: (088) 269-2888

- ROUTE MOBIEL
  Postbus 2891
  3500 GW Utrecht
  General information: tel: 0800-0504 (free of charge)
  Car assistance: tel: (026) 355-3300

Driving an automobile in the Netherlands:
- RDW (Rijksdienst voor Wegverkeer)
  Tel: 0900-0739
  Website: http://www.rdw.nl

Trade Union Issues
- FNV is the largest trade union organisation in the Netherlands
  ABVAKABO FNV (head office)
  Boerhaavelaan 1
  2713 HA Zoetermeer
  Tel: (0900) 228-2522

CAREER SERVICES
Look in the *Yellow Pages* under *Loopbaanbegeleiding* or search the Internet, eg via Google for 'career services Netherlands'.

Legal Aid Agencies
- There is an emergency number for legal aid:
  tel: (020) 616-0120.
- Legal advice is available, for a reasonable fee, at the Rechtshulp, found throughout the country. Its contact number in Rotterdam is (010) 443-2100 and its website (in Dutch only) is http://www.rechtshulpnederland.nl. With a Dutch friend to help you, this is a very good place to begin.
- If you are a member of the ANWB, you can get from it free legal advice about traffic, tourism, and recreation.

FURTHER READING

Much of what has been written in English about the Netherlands (or translated from Dutch into English) are academic, business or technical works designed primarily for the specialist. The following books, however, are easy and enjoyable to read.

The Embarrassment of Riches: An Interpretation of Dutch Culture in the Golden Age. Simon Schama. New York: Vintage: 1997.

Investment in the Netherlands. KPMG International Business Support (Amstelveen) 2005.

The Low Sky: Understanding the Dutch. Han van der Horst. Trans. Andy Brown. The Hague: Scriptum Books/ Nuffic, 2001.

The Netherlands in Brief. Foreign Information Service, Ministry of Foreign Affairs. The Hague, 1994.

Michelin Guides: Netherlands. Michelin Tyre, Tourism Department, Watford (Herts). Look for the latest edition.

The UnDutchables: An Observation of the Netherlands, Its Culture and Its Inhabitants. Colin White and Laurie Boucke. Montrose, CA: White-Boucke Publishing, 2001 (4th ed).

The Xenophobe's Guide to the Dutch. Rodney Bolt. London: Oval Books, 1999.

ABOUT THE AUTHORS

Hunt Janin is an American writer now living in south-western France. He specialises in international issues and has written or co-authored nine books and nine magazine articles.

Hunt has an MA in political science from the University of California (Berkeley) and was a Fellow at Harvard University and a Tutor at the Civil Service College in London. For 25 years, he served as a diplomat in Washington, DC, India, Ghana, Lebanon, Saudi Arabia and Nepal. He is married to Corinne Janin-Nuis, a former member of the Netherlands Foreign Service. Thanks to her, he has many Dutch friends and visits the Netherlands frequently. In the future, Hunt and Corrine plan to spend part of each year in the Netherlands.

Ria van Eil spent the first 22 years of her life in Amsterdam, where she met her husband Adrian, an officer with the Netherlands Foreign Service. For 23 years, she served with him abroad in Switzerland, Belgium, the US, France, Russia, the UK and Suriname. Deeply interested in peoples, languages and cultures, she managed to get work permits for every country in which they served. Capitalising on a life-long interest in France, she graduated in French language and literature during their time in Paris. Ria and Adrian now live in The Hague. In the near future, they intend to move to France, where Ria now spends part of each year.

Ria and Hunt met at the Netherlands Embassy in London in 1991, where Hunt's wife Corinne was also posted.

222

INDEX

Titles in the CultureShock! series:

Argentina	France	Russia
Australia	Germany	San Francisco
Austria	Hawaii	Saudi Arabia
Bahrain	Hong Kong	Scotland
Beijing	Hungary	Shanghai
Belgium	India	Singapore
Bolivia	Ireland	South Africa
Borneo	Italy	Spain
Brazil	Jakarta	Sri Lanka
Britain	Japan	Sweden
Bulgaria	Korea	Switzerland
Cambodia	Laos	Syria
Canada	London	Taiwan
Chicago	Malaysia	Thailand
Chile	Mauritius	Tokyo
China	Morocco	Turkey
Costa Rica	Munich	United Arab
Cuba	Myanmar	Emirates
Czech Republic	Netherlands	USA
Denmark	New Zealand	Vancouver
Ecuador	Paris	Venezuela
Egypt	Philippines	
Finland	Portugal	

For more information about any of these titles, please contact any of our Marshall Cavendish offices around the world (listed on page ii) or visit our website at:

www.marshallcavendish.com/genref